Easy 1-2-3 Macros

Don Roche, Jr.

Easy 1-2-3 Macros

Copyright© 1992 by Que® Corporation

All rights reserved. Printed in the United States of America. No part of this book may be used or reproduced in any form or by any means, or stored in a database or retrieval system, without prior written permission of the publisher except in the case of brief quotations embodied in critical articles and reviews. Making copies of any part of this book for any purpose other than your own personal use is a violation of United States copyright laws. For information, address Que Corporation, 11711 N. College Ave., Carmel, IN 46032.

Library of Congress Catalog: 92-61985

ISBN: 1-56529-105-0

This book is sold *as is*, without warranty of any kind, either express or implied, respecting the contents of this book, including but not limited to implied warranties for the book's quality, performance, merchantability, or fitness for any particular purpose. Neither Que Corporation nor its dealers or distributors shall be liable to the purchaser or any other person or entity with respect to any liability, loss, or damage caused or alleged to have been caused directly or indirectly by this book.

95 94 93 92   4 3 2 1

Interpretation of the printing code: the rightmost double-digit number is the year of the book's printing; the rightmost single-digit number, the number of the book's printing. For example, a printing code of 92-1 shows that the first printing of the book occurred in 1992.

Screen reproductions in this book were created with Collage Plus from Inner Media, Inc., Hollis, NH.

Publisher: Lloyd J. Short

Associate Publisher: Rick Ranucci

Product Development Manager: Thomas H. Bennett

Book Designer: Scott Cook

Production Analyst: Mary Beth Wakefield

Graphic Imaging Specialist: Dennis Sheehan

Production Team: Debra Adams, Jeff Baker, Claudia Bell, Bob LaRoche, Caroline Roop, Susan Vandewalle, Lisa Wilson, Phil Worthington

Dedication

This book is dedicated to my parents-in-law, Paul and Janice Hutko, two wonderful people who dedicate their lives to the challenge of educating people. I know few people whom I respect more.

Credits

Title Manager
Joyce Nielsen

Production Editor
Anne Owen

Copy Editor
Fran Blauw

Acquisitions Editor
Tim Ryan

Technical Editor
Dave Williamson

Editorial Assistance
Betsy Brown

Composed in *Utopia* and *MCPdigital* by Que Corporation

About the Author

Don Roche, Jr. is the Spreadsheet Title Manager at Que Corporation. Formerly an independent personal computer consultant and a senior trainer and curriculum developer, he is the author of *Quattro Pro 4 QuickStart* and *Excel 4 for Windows Quick Reference*. He is a contributing author to *1-2-3 Power Macros*, *Using 1-2-3 for Windows*, *Using 1-2-3 Release 2.4*, Special Edition, and *Using Ami Pro 3*, Special Edition. Mr. Roche also has performed technical edits of more than 15 computer books, including *Using Symphony*, Special Edition. He has a degree in English from Boston College.

Acknowledgments

This book, like so many other books, is the work of many people. I'd like to thank the following people for their work on *Easy 1-2-3 Macros*:

Joyce Nielsen, Senior Product Development Specialist, whose dedication and content contributions ensured a great book. Joyce, a spreadhseet guru, was enormously helpful in identifying the macro elements to include in this book.

Tim Ryan, Acquisitions Editor, for giving me a chance to write this book. **Tim Ryan**, **Chuck Stewart**, Que Title Manager, and **Elden Nelson**, Senior Writer for WordPerfect Publishing, were instrumental in determining the tone and direction of the book.

Anne Owen, Production Editor, for her insightful questions and superb edit of the book.

Fran Blauw, Copy Editor, who helped Anne ensure a high-quality final manuscript.

Scott Cook, Book Designer, for all his hard work in designing this book.

David Williamson, Technical Editor, for his excellent technical edit of this book.

Trademarks

All terms mentioned in this book that are known to be trademarks or service marks have been appropriately capitalized. Que cannot attest to the accuracy of this information. Use of a term in this book should not be regarded as affecting the validity of any trademark or service mark.

Contents at a Glance

Introduction 1

I Getting Started with 1-2-3 Macros

1 What Are Macros? 7
2 Writing Your First Macro 11
3 Creating One-Line Macros That Erase Data 23
4 Creating Simple Macros That Change
   Column Widths 31
5 Creating Simple Macros That Format Numbers 43

II Testing and Automating Macros

6 Testing Macros 57
7 Recording Macro Keystrokes 69
8 Using the Macro Library Manager
   with Release 2.x 87

III Advancing Your Use of Macros

9 Creating Macros That Perform Multiple Tasks 103
10 Moving to the Next Level 111
11 Pausing a Macro 115
12 Prompting a User for Input 135
13 Testing for Worksheet Conditions 143
14 Making the Computer Beep 153

Table of Contents

Introduction 1
    Who Should Buy This Book? 2
    What Versions of 1-2-3 Are Covered? 2
    Special Conventions Used in This Book 3
    How Can You Learn More about 1-2-3 and
        1-2-3 Macros? 4

I Getting Started with 1-2-3 Macros

1 What Are Macros? 7
    Defining Macros 8
    Using Macros 9
    From Here... 9

2 Writing Your First Macro 11
    Writing a Simple Macro To Enter Your Name 12
        Planning the Macro 12
        Placing the Macro 13
        Entering the Macro 14
        Naming the Macro 15
        Documenting the Macro 16
        Running the Macro 17
    Guidelines for Creating Macros 18
    Guidelines for Naming and Running Macros 19
        Alt-*letter* Macros 20
        Macros with Descriptive Names 21
    From Here... 22

3 Writing One-Line Macros That Erase Data 23
    A Macro That Erases Data in a Single Cell 24
    A Macro That Erases a Range of Data 27
    From Here... 30

4 Creating Simple Macros That Change Column Widths 31

A Macro That Changes the Width of a Single Column 32
A Macro That Changes the Width of Multiple Columns 36
A Macro That Changes the Width of All Columns 39
From Here... 42

5 Creating Simple Macros That Format Numbers 43

A Macro That Formats a Range as Comma with 2 Decimal Places 44
A Macro That Formats a Range as Currency with 0 Decimal Places 47
A Macro That Changes the Default Cell Format to Currency with 2 Decimal Places 49
From Here... 53

II Testing and Automating Macros

6 Testing Macros 57

Using STEP Mode To Test Macros 58
    Stepping through a Macro That Erases Data 59
    Stepping through a Macro That Formats Data 64
Avoiding Common Macro Errors 66
Using Undo To Reverse the Effects of a Macro 67
From Here... 68

7 Recording Macro Keystrokes 69

Defining the Learn Range 70
Activating LEARN Mode 71
Recording a Macro That Types Your Name, City, and State 72
Recording a Macro That Saves a Worksheet 76
Recording a Macro That Changes the File Directory ... 78
Recording a Macro in 1-2-3 Release 3.x 80
From Here... 85

8 Using the Macro Library Manager with Release 2.x 87

Adding the Macro Library Manager 88
Creating a Macro Library 91
Editing a Macro Library 94
Removing a Macro Library from Memory 97
Loading a Macro Library into Memory 98
From Here... 99

III Advancing Your Use of Macros

9 Creating Macros That Perform Multiple Tasks 103

A Macro That Enters Your Name and Address 104
A Macro That Prints a Worksheet with a
   Footer and Page Number 107
From Here... 110

10 Moving to the Next Level 111

What Are the Advanced Macro Commands? 112
Rules for the Advanced Macro Commands 112
From Here... 114

11 Pausing a Macro 115

Pausing a Macro To Erase Cells 116
Pausing a Macro To Format Numbers 119
Pausing a Macro To Change Column Widths 122
Creating a User Input Macro 125
From Here... 133

12 Prompting the User for Input 135

Modifying the User Input Macro 136
   Understanding the {GETLABEL} Command 137
   Understanding the {IF} Command 138
   Creating and Running the Macro 139
From Here... 142

xi

13 Testing for Worksheet Conditions 143

Using Operators with the {IF} Command 144
Using @CELLPOINTER with the {IF} Command 147
From Here... 151

14 Making the Computer Beep 153

Using the {BEEP} Command 154
Using the {BEEP} Command
    in a User Input Macro 156

Introduction

Lotus 1-2-3 is one of the most popular PC spreadsheet programs ever created. Many companies control their operating budget and invoicing by using 1-2-3, and millions of people use 1-2-3 daily.

Most 1-2-3 users have heard about macros, but they aren't sure what macros are or what they do. And that's a shame, because macros are one of the most useful features 1-2-3 offers! *Easy 1-2-3 Macros* teaches you how to create and use macros.

As the title of this book implies, we're going to take the *easy* road to learning macros. We're going to start right from the beginning by defining a macro, explaining macro guidelines in detail, and then progress to creating and running our own macros. You will be surprised at how easy it is to create and run your own macro!

Who Should Buy This Book?

If you're interested in learning how to create Lotus 1-2-3 macros, *Easy 1-2-3 Macros* is for you. This book uses a tutorial approach with several step-by-step examples and takes a light hearted, fun approach to learning macros.

If you're thinking about learning macros, you probably have some experience with 1-2-3. This book assumes very little, but it does assume that you know basic 1-2-3 tasks, such as retrieving and saving worksheets. *You don't need to be a 1-2-3 guru to learn macros!* Far from it! Macros make working with 1-2-3 easier for anyone; if you know a little about 1-2-3, you will benefit by reading this book.

> **NOTE**
>
> In this book, 1-2-3 Release 2.x refers to 1-2-3 Releases 2.01, 2.2, 2.3, and 2.4; 1-2-3 Release 3.x refers to 1-2-3 Releases 3.0, 3.1, and 3.1+.

What Versions of 1-2-3 Are Covered?

This book covers Lotus 1-2-3 for DOS Releases 2.x and 3.x. Each macro discussed in this book will run in all 1-2-3 for DOS versions. Macro procedures that differ between versions of 1-2-3 include a notation to that effect.

Special Conventions Used in This Book

Easy 1-2-3 Macros uses certain conventions to help you learn the techniques and macros described in the text. This section explains these conventions.

Special typefaces in *Easy 1-2-3 Macros* include the following:

Typeface	Meaning
italics	New terms or phrases when they are defined; macro command arguments
Boldface Blue	Information you're asked to type, including the first character of 1-2-3 menu options and the slash (/) that brings up the 1-2-3 main menu
`special typeface`	Words that appear on-screen or in a figure; menu command prompts

When two keys are separated by a hyphen, such as Ctrl-Break, you press and hold down the first key and then press the second key.

Conventions that pertain specifically to macros include the following:

- Alt-*letter* macro names appear with a backslash (\) and single-character names in lowercase, such as \a. The \ means that you hold down the Alt key while you press the letter A.

- 1-2-3 menu keystrokes within macros appear in lowercase: `/rfc`.

- In a macro, the Enter key is represented by the tilde (~).

- 1-2-3 advanced macro commands (discussed in the last few chapters of this book) appear in uppercase and are enclosed within braces, such as {GETLABEL}.

This "butler" icon appears in the margin next to each numbered step macro example. We use this analogy because the macros you create in this book automate tasks for you, just as a butler does things for you.

> **NOTE**
>
> This paragraph format indicates additional information that may help you avoid problems and information that should be considered in using the described features.

OOPS! This paragraph format warns you of hazardous procedures or things to watch out for. This "butler tripping" icon appears in the margin beside each **OOPS!** box.

How Can You Learn More about 1-2-3 and 1-2-3 Macros?

After you learn the fundamentals of macros, you can benefit by picking up Que's *1-2-3 Power Macros*. This book takes you to the next level of using macros and is written for those 1-2-3 users who are already comfortable with writing simple macros. This book includes a disk containing over 150 macros and macro applications.

You also can benefit from Que's comprehensive 1-2-3 reference books: *Using 1-2-3 Release 2.4*, Special Edition (covering 1-2-3 Releases 2.01, 2.2, 2.3, and 2.4), or *Using 1-2-3 Release 3.1+*, Special Edition (covering 1-2-3 Releases 3.0, 3.1, and 3.1+). Because macros automate 1-2-3 tasks, obtaining a complete reference can be invaluable.

You can find these books in bookstores worldwide. In the United States, you can call Que at 1-800-428-5331 to order books or to obtain more information.

Getting Started with 1-2-3 Macros

PART

I

ENTER COMM
RANGE ALT
LABEL ENTE
GETLABEL RA
ENTER MAC
COMMAND

What Are Macros?

CHAPTER 1

Easy 1-2-3 Macros

This book shows you how to use one of the best features 1-2-3 offers—macros. You will learn how to create, name, document, and run a macro. This book takes a very easy-going approach to learning macros and contains many illustrative figures to help you along. *Easy 1-2-3 Macros* book is a tutorial, so you can always go back and review as you need to.

By automating 1-2-3 operations, a macro performs tasks so you don't have to. Macros can save you time and energy because they quickly accomplish tasks you perform frequently, such as erasing data, widening a column, or changing a label alignment. All you have to do is tell 1-2-3 to run the macro, and the macro does all the work.

Defining Macros

A *macro* is a series of keystrokes that 1-2-3 executes for you. A macro is like a butler. If you hire a butler, you show him certain tasks you want him to perform. For instance, you can show the butler the steps necessary to make your breakfast:

1. Take out a cereal bowl.
2. Pour cereal into the bowl.
3. Pour milk into the bowl.
4. Put a spoon in the bowl.
5. Take out a glass.
6. Pour orange juice into the glass.

After you show the butler what to do, he performs the task you ask him to perform when you ring for him. When you ask him to get breakfast, you expect him to follow the preceding steps. You simply sit back and continue to read the morning paper while you sip a fresh cup of coffee.

Macros act as a "butler" for your 1-2-3 worksheet. When you run a macro, it performs whatever task you told it to perform when you created the macro. You just sit back and wait for the macro to finish running. Because macros are very fast, you probably won't have time for the paper and a cup of coffee!

Using Macros

Using macros saves you time and effort. Macros execute very quickly and perform operations much faster than you can manually. Macros can automate almost any task you perform with 1-2-3, and they enable you to work efficiently and effectively with a worksheet.

Macros take the drudgery out of repetitive tasks because macros repeat the same keystrokes as many times as necessary. Each time you need to perform the task, simply run the macro. Macros also eliminate typing mistakes because after you create and run the macro correctly, you avoid pressing the wrong key.

Macros are among the most useful 1-2-3 capabilities you will ever learn. Because you can automate almost any task by using a macro, its potential is immense. I guarantee that when you learn how to create and run 1-2-3 macros, you will wish you had learned about macros sooner!

From Here...

Now that you have an idea of what macros are, let's learn about some of the guidelines for using macros, discussed in the next chapter. Just as a butler has certain rules to follow, a macro also has certain rules to follow. Don't worry—these rules aren't *too* strict, but you do need to keep a few guidelines in mind when working with macros.

Easy 1-2-3 Macros

Writing Your First Macro

CHAPTER 2

Easy 1-2-3 Macros

In this chapter, you create and run your first macro! By creating and running your first macro, you begin to see how you can make 1-2-3 macros work for you. Your first macro types your name and enters it into the worksheet. Each time you run the macro, your name is entered into the highlighted cell.

A couple of thoughts before we begin our adventure. First, have no fears; this is a tutorial, and I thoroughly explain each step required to create and run the macro. Second, I want to point out the general steps involved in creating a macro.

These steps include the following:

1. Plan what the macro will do.
2. Select an area of the worksheet for placing the macro instructions.
3. Enter the macro instructions into the worksheet.
4. Name the macro.
5. Document the macro.
6. Run the macro.

In the next few sections, you will follow these steps to create and run your first macro. OK—strap on your parachute. It's time to jump!

Writing a Simple Macro To Enter Your Name

You can use your first macro—the macro to enter your name—when you need to put your name on a worksheet so co-workers know who created the worksheet. You also can use this macro to add your name to a note in a worksheet. You can change the macro to enter your company name, your division, your employee number, or whatever single piece of information you need in your worksheet.

Planning the Macro

The first thing we need to do is plan the macro. That's easy for this macro. Because the macro is going to type your name, you really don't need a planning stage (unless, of course, a large rock was accidentally dropped on your head this morning, and you can't remember your name; if that's the case, you probably shouldn't be trying to learn

Writing Your First Macro

macros this morning anyway!). Planning is very important, however, for a macro that performs multiple tasks because these tasks usually must be performed in a certain order.

Placing the Macro

Macros need to be written in an area of the worksheet separate from your data. You want to make sure that your macro isn't interfering with entering and editing data. A good rule of thumb is to set the standard macro layout starting in column AA because most worksheet data fits within the 26 columns that precede column AA. If your worksheet or database extends into column AA, your macro should begin in a column *farther* to the right of column AA, such as column BA.

You can have multiple macros in one worksheet. Typically, you will have several macros in a single worksheet. When you save a file that has macros, you save the macros with that file. The file *owns* the macros and no other file. However, you can combine the macros from one file to another, and then both files contain the macros.

Release 3.x can have multiple sheets within one file. For example, if you insert two sheets, you have sheets A, B, and C in one file. If you're using Release 3.x, you put your macros in a separate sheet. If your macros are in their own sheet, separate from the data sheet, you don't have to worry about your macros interfering when you enter or edit data.

To create the standard layout for your macro, first move the cell pointer to cell AA1. The standard macro layout involves three columns, with the column headings NAME, MACROS, and DESCRIPTION. The first column, NAME, is for the name of the macro. The second column, MACRO, is for the keystrokes and commands the macro executes. The third column, DESCRIPTION, is for the description of the macro instructions. These headings aren't necessary, but documenting your macros with headings makes the macro much easier for others to understand.

OK, let's create the layout for our macro by following these steps:

1. Enter the heading NAME in cell AA1, the heading MACRO in cell AB1, and the heading DESCRIPTION in cell AC1.
2. Underline each of these labels.
3. Select /Worksheet Column Set-Width.
4. Widen column AB to 25; then widen column AC to 35.

Easy 1-2-3 Macros

Your worksheet should look like figure 2.1.

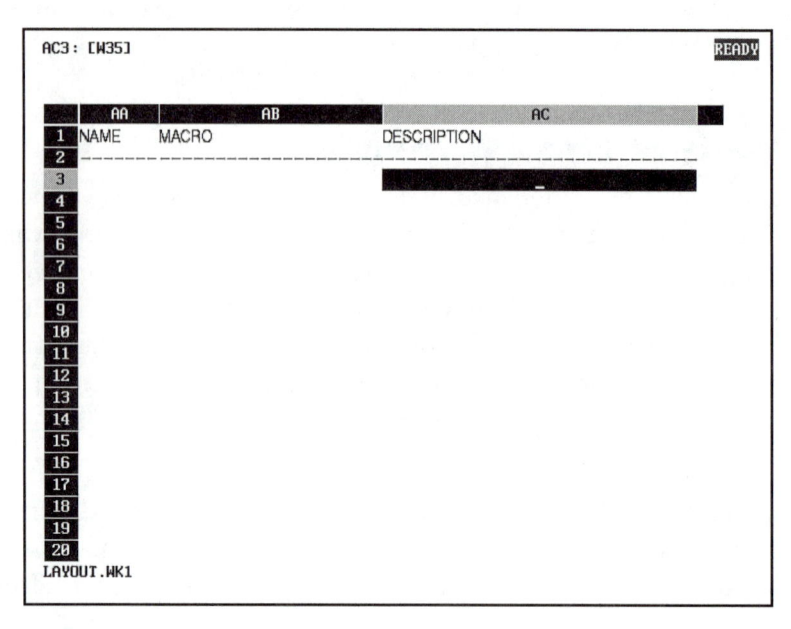

Fig. 2.1 The standard macro layout.

To save this file, select **/F**ile **S**ave and enter the file name **LAYOUT**. Saving the standard layout enables you to retrieve it when you need to create macros.

Now that we have the standard layout set up, we can begin entering our macro.

Entering the Macro

The macro to type your name is a simple, one-line macro. Even though it's a one-line macro, 1-2-3 has multiple instructions to execute when the macro runs. The number of instructions depends on your name. 1-2-3 executes 14 keystrokes to enter *my* name: one keystroke for each letter (including spaces)—**Don Roche Jr.**, and one keystroke to press **Enter**.

Let's go ahead and enter the macro. Follow these steps:

1. Move the cell pointer to cell AB3, the first cell in the MACRO column.

2. Type your name, followed by a tilde (~).

> **NOTE**
>
> The Enter key is represented by the tilde (~) in a macro. Each time you need the macro to press **Enter**, you place a tilde in the macro. You probably haven't used the tilde before, but trust me—it's there somewhere on your keyboard (usually in the upper left corner of the keyboard).

Writing Your First Macro

I type the following:

   Don Roche Jr.~

You type your name—*Bill Smith* or *Sally Sue Jones,* or whatever your name happens to be—followed by a tilde. What I don't want you to type are the letters *your name.* (I only include this reminder for those of you who haven't had three or four cups of coffee, a handful of vitamins, or whatever it is that opens your eyes in the morning.)

3. Press Enter.

Figure 2.2 shows the macro to enter my name.

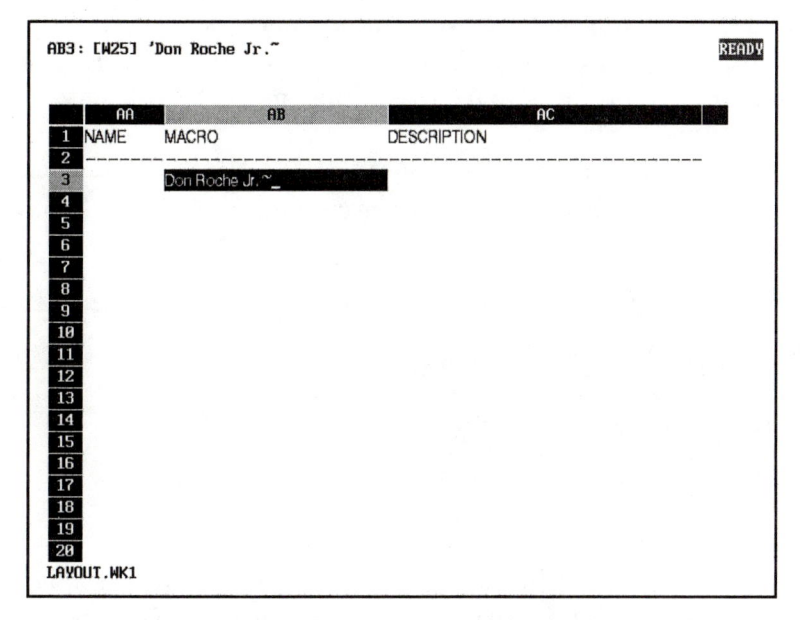

Fig. 2.2   The macro to enter my name in the current cell.

Now you have finished creating the macro to enter your name. Nice job! Because we haven't named the macro yet, we can't run it. So next, we'll name the macro.

Naming the Macro

Let's name this macro \n. The \n macro is an Alt-*letter* macro name, which means that we can run the macro by holding down the Alt key and pressing the letter N (Alt-N). The backslash (\) in the macro name represents the Alt key.

Easy 1-2-3 Macros

To enter the name of the macro into the worksheet, follow these steps:

1. Move the cell pointer to cell AA3.

2. Type `'\n` (don't forget the apostrophe!) and press Enter.

Entering \n into cell AA3 doesn't actually name the macro so we can run it. A second step, which we will perform next, establishes the macro name.

OOPS! If you don't enter an apostrophe before an Alt-*letter* macro name, you get the letter *n* repeating the width of cell AA3. In 1-2-3, the backslash key is the repeat character key and often is used to underline cells by entering \-. Because we want the actual characters \n entered into the cell, we must precede the characters with an apostrophe. This procedure ensures that 1-2-3 recognizes this entry as a label entry.

Now, we must use the /Range Name Create command to establish the macro name as \n.

Follow these steps:

1. Move the cell pointer to cell AB3.

2. Select /Range Name Create.

3. Type \n at the `Enter Range Name:` prompt.

4. Press Enter to establish cell AB3 as the cell to name \n.

We also can use the /Range Name Labels Right command to establish the macro name as \n. This command applies the label in the highlighted cell as a range name of the cell directly to its right. If we place the cell pointer in cell AA3 and select /Range Name Labels Right, our macro cell, AB3, is named \n.

The macro now has the name \n assigned to it. We can run the macro at this point, but we still have some work to do before the macro is complete. We need to document the macro. You document the macro in the DESCRIPTION column.

Documenting the Macro

Documenting macros is important so that anyone using the macro at a later date (including yourself!) knows exactly what the macro does. Documenting the macro also makes it easier for you to edit the macro.

Writing Your First Macro

Documenting this macro is very easy. The macro types your name when the macro executes (the macro description states this).

To document your macro, follow these steps:

1. Move the cell pointer to cell AC3.

2. Type **Macro to type my name** and press **Enter**.

Figure 2.3 shows the macro with the description entered.

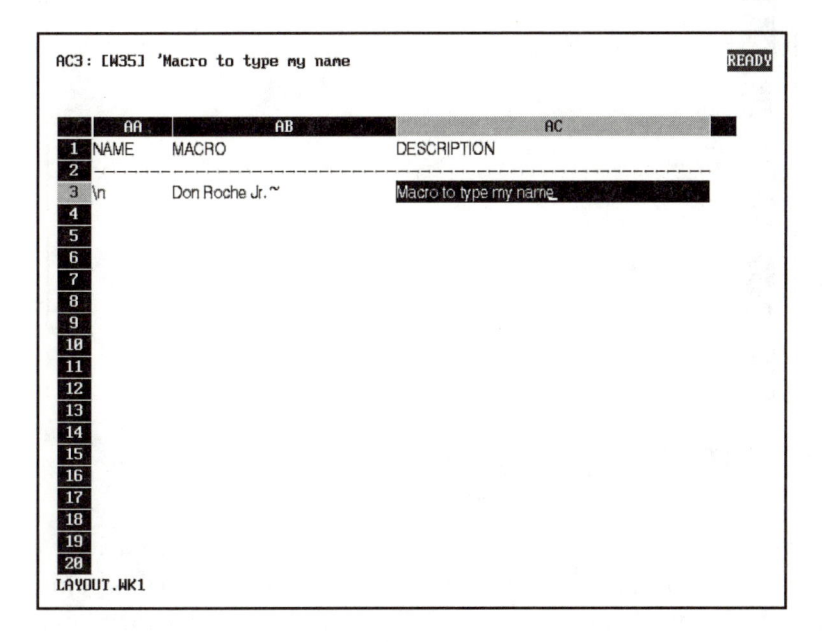

Fig. 2.3 The documented \n macro.

Now we can run the macro!

Running the Macro

Because this macro is named \n, we can run the macro by pressing the **Alt** key and the letter **N** (**Alt-N**). First, we need to move to the desired location for your name. Let's move to cell A1 and run the macro.

To run the \n macro, follow these steps:

1. Move the cell pointer to cell A1.

2. Press and hold the **Alt** key, then press the letter **N**.

17

Figure 2.4 shows the result of running the macro. The name now appears in cell A1. Now save the file containing the macro with the file name MYNAME.

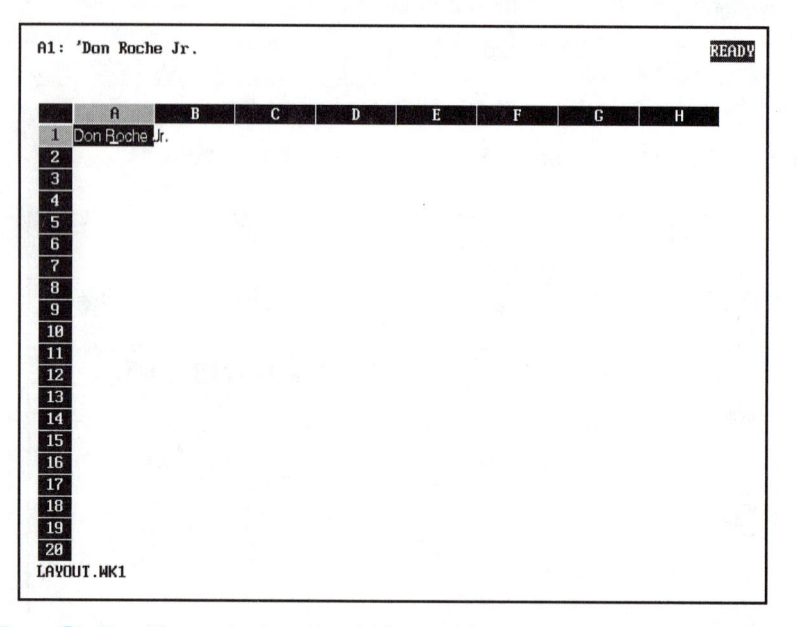

Fig. 2.4 The result of running the \n macro.

There you have it. You're now officially a Lotus 1-2-3 macro writer. Congratulations! Everything you learn about macros from this point forward follows similar procedures. So onward, brave macro writer...

The sections that follow explain in a little more detail the guidelines for creating, naming, and running macros.

Guidelines for Creating Macros

You must follow certain conventions to ensure the successful operation of 1-2-3 macros. For example, when you type a macro into a worksheet, each cell of the macro should be preceded by an apostrophe (') because all macro cells must be labels. A *label* is anything that isn't a number or formula. The apostrophe forces 1-2-3 to recognize what is entered into the cell as a label. These labels contain the keys to press or the commands to execute when the macro is run. The apostrophe ensures that a cell entry is a label.

Writing Your First Macro

To illustrate the necessity of the apostrophe, let's say you want to create a macro to erase a cell. The macro must execute the 1-2-3 command, /**R**ange **E**rase, to erase a cell. Because the /**R**ange **E**rase command is a menu command, the macro must bring up the menu, select **R**ange, select **E**rase, and finally press **Enter**. The macro must include the slash command (/), which is the command to bring up the menu.

Because the menu appears when you press the slash key (/), you must use an apostrophe to precede the slash used in the macro. If you don't precede the slash command with an apostrophe, each time you press the slash key to include it in the macro, the menu appears! You may think to yourself, "I know this is the right key, but why doesn't it appear in the cell?" You press the slash key harder, believing you aren't pressing the key vigorously enough. Next you pound on the slash key, convinced that the slash only types into the cell if you beat the heck out of the key. Sorry, no dice. Remember, you can't type the slash key into a cell unless you precede the slash by an apostrophe.

You can select any 1-2-3 menu command by pressing the first letter of the command. You can choose **R**ange, for example, by pressing the letter **R**. You can choose **E**rase by pressing the letter **E**. Every 1-2-3 menu command has a unique first letter. Always use the first letter of the menu command when you create a macro that includes a menu command.

> **NOTE**
>
> You can type a lowercase or uppercase letter to make a menu selection. In this book, we use lowercase letters within macros to indicate menu commands.

Guidelines for Naming and Running Macros

As you learned previously in this chapter, macros must have a name before you can run them. You have two options for naming your macros. You can give macros a name consisting of a backslash plus a single letter, or you can give macros a descriptive name of up to 15 characters. (Descriptive names are available in 1-2-3 Release 2.2 and higher.) The \h macro in figure 2.5 shows a macro with an Alt-*letter* name. You can run this macro by pressing the **Alt** key and the letter **H** (**Alt-H**).

The backslash (\) plus a single letter gives you a quicker way to run a macro. It is, however, more difficult to remember the macro task since all you have in the name is a single letter. A macro named Print_Budget tells you exactly what the macro does. A macro named \p doesn't tell you exactly what the macro does.

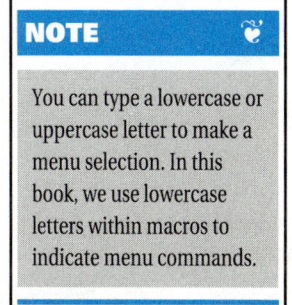

19

Easy 1-2-3 Macros

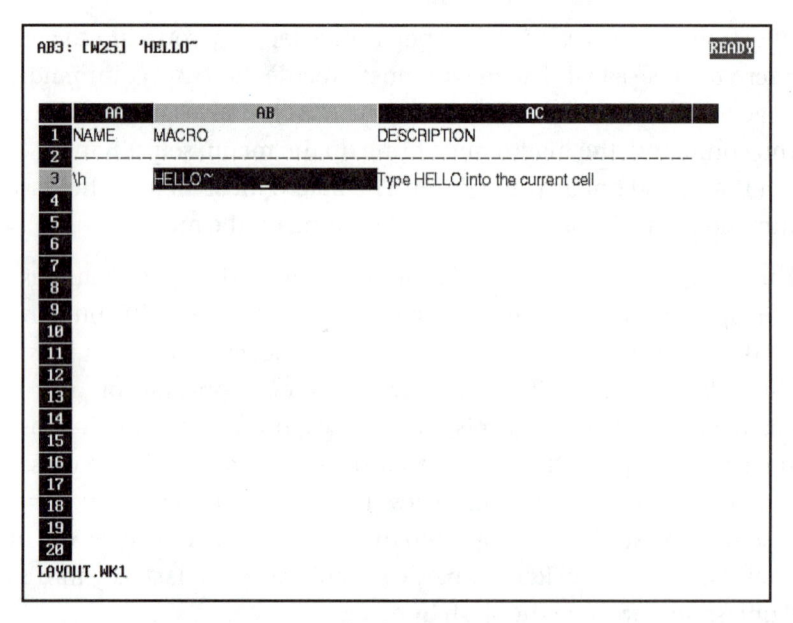

```
AB3: [W25] 'HELLO~                                              READY

        AA              AB                      AC
  1  NAME           MACRO                   DESCRIPTION
  2  ─────────────────────────────────────────────────────
  3  \h             HELLO~     _            Type HELLO into the current cell
  4
  5
  6
  7
  8
  9
 10
 11
 12
 13
 14
 15
 16
 17
 18
 19
 20
LAYOUT.WK1
```

Fig. 2.5 A macro with an Alt-*letter* name.

When you run a macro, 1-2-3 reads the instructions for the macro, and the keys and commands are activated in the order in which they appear in the macro. The macro stops running when all the commands are executed. The macro to enter **HELLO** into a cell, shown in figure 2.5, executes six keystroke instructions: five instructions for typing out letters and one instruction (the tilde) for pressing the **Enter** key. Each keystroke is a separate instruction.

Alt-*letter* Macros

One way to understand the benefits of an Alt-*letter* macro is to consider the number of times you perform specific tasks, such as erase cells, format numbers, widen columns, print worksheets, or save and retrieve files. In each case, you perform the operation by typing a series of keystrokes. Sometimes, the operation requires a rather lengthy series of keystrokes. By using an Alt-*letter* macro, however, you can reduce the number of keystrokes required by many operations to a two-keystroke combination. That is, you can execute the macro by holding down the **Alt** key and pressing the letter that represents the macro's name. To run the macro in figure 2.5, for example, you hold down the **Alt** key and press the letter **H**. Macros executed in this manner are called "Alt-*letter*" macros. Note that throughout this book (as in the 1-2-3 documentation), the Alt key is represented by the backslash character (\) in Alt-*letter* macro names. Because the alphabet consists of 26 letters, 26 possible Alt-*letter* macros are possible in one worksheet.

Writing Your First Macro

OOPS! Make sure that you use the backslash key (\) and not the slash key (/) when naming your Alt-*letter* macros. If you use the slash key (/), the macro doesn't run when you press **Alt** and the designated letter.

Macros with Descriptive Names

In 1-2-3 Release 2.2 and higher, you can name your macros with a descriptive name, such as RANGE_ERASE (for a macro that erases a cell) or PRINT_BUDGET (for a macro that prints your company's budget worksheet) instead of an Alt-*letter* name. The macro names can be up to 15 characters. Obviously, descriptive macro names more clearly describe the actions of macros than do Alt-*letter* macros, such as \e or \p. The only difference between using a descriptive name and an Alt-*letter* name, besides the obvious descriptive difference, is the way you run the macro. The same macro commands still run either way. You still name the macro by using the **/R**ange **N**ame **C**reate command.

You run macros with descriptive names by pressing **Alt-F3** (the Run key) and typing the macro name or selecting the macro from the list of names that appears.

Figure 2.6 shows a macro with a descriptive name.

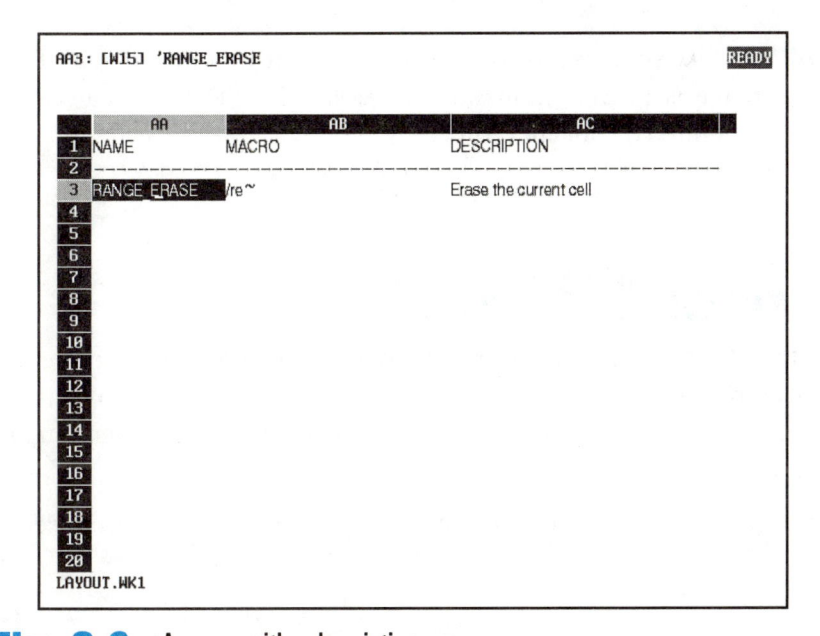

> **NOTE**
>
> Because the Run key is not available in Release 2.01, all macros executed in that Release must be Alt-*letter* macros.

Fig. 2.6 A macro with a descriptive name.

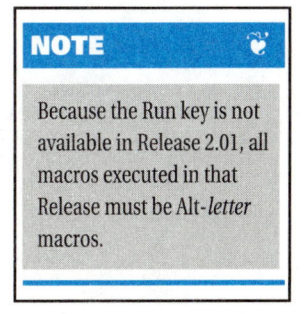

21

Easy 1-2-3 Macros

When you press **Alt-F3** (Run), the prompt `Select the macro to run:` appears in the upper left corner of the screen (see fig. 2.7). You then highlight the name of the macro you want to run and press **Enter**.

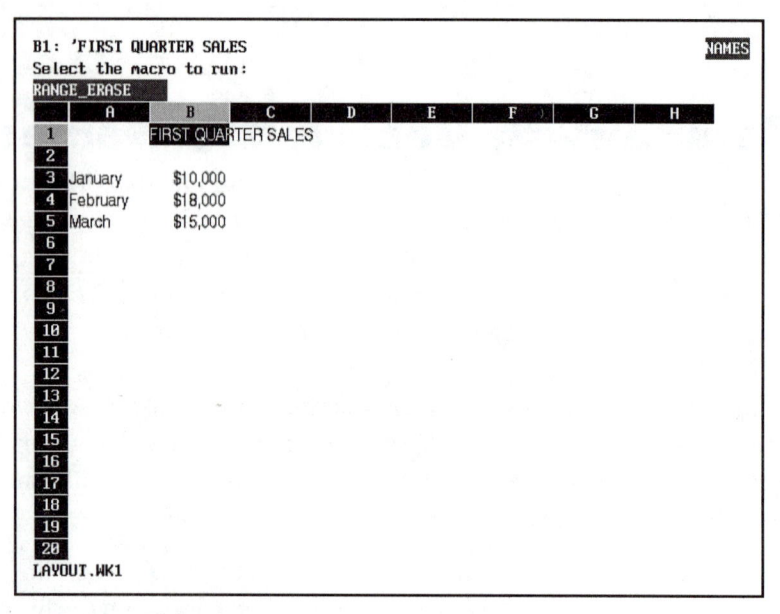

Fig. 2.7   The prompt to select a macro to run.

OOPS! Make sure that you don't use a name for your macro that's the same name as a 1-2-3 command, such as CALC or EDIT. This can cause problems when the macro is run.

From Here...

In this chapter, you created a macro to write your name at the current cell pointer address. You planned the macro, placed the macro, entered the macro, named the macro, documented the macro, and then ran the macro. Good job!

In the next chapter, we create simple macros that erase data from cells.

Writing One-Line Macros That Erase Data

CHAPTER 3

Easy 1-2-3 Macros

> **NOTE**
>
> In 1-2-3 Releases 2.3 and 2.4 only, you can press the Del key to delete the contents of the current cell (which is quicker than creating a macro that requires two keystrokes). Therefore, you should only need to create a macro to erase the contents of the current cell if you are using 1-2-3 Releases 2.01, 2.2, or 3.x.

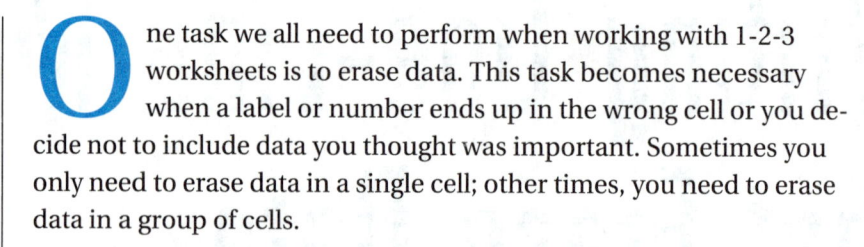

One task we all need to perform when working with 1-2-3 worksheets is to erase data. This task becomes necessary when a label or number ends up in the wrong cell or you decide not to include data you thought was important. Sometimes you only need to erase data in a single cell; other times, you need to erase data in a group of cells.

In this chapter, we will write two macros. The first macro erases data in a single cell. The second macro erases data in a group of cells. Repetitive tasks like erasing data are excellent examples of when to use a macro. Because a macro performs the task quicker than you can manually, you save time. Because you only have to press two keys to run a macro (if you name the macro by using the Alt-*letter* method, as we will), using a macro takes some of the tedium out of the repetitive tasks.

A Macro That Erases Data in a Single Cell

In Chapter 2, the first macro you wrote typed your name into the current cell (the highlighted cell). The following macro will erase the data in the current cell.

First, let's identify the *manual* steps required to erase the data in the current cell:

1. Press **/** to bring up the main 1-2-3 menu.
2. Select **R**ange.
3. Select **E**rase.
4. Press **Enter**.

The preceding steps are the steps we tell the macro to perform.

In Chapter 2, we built the standard macro layout and saved it with the file name LAYOUT. Let's retrieve the LAYOUT worksheet now so that we don't have to build the layout again for this macro. Because we want to preserve the file LAYOUT for future use, save the file with the name ERASE. We will write the new macro in this file.

Now we're ready to write the first macro.

Writing One-Line Macros That Erase Data

To create the macro to erase the data in the current cell, follow these steps:

1. Move the cell pointer to cell AB3 (the first cell in the MACRO column).

2. Type **'/re~** (don't forget the apostrophe!) and press **Enter**.

   /re~ are the macro instructions to erase the data in the current cell.

3. To name the macro, move the cell pointer to cell AA3 (the first cell in the NAME column).

4. Type **'\e** and press **Enter**.

   Because this macro erases data, we will name it \e (for *erase*).

5. Select **/R**ange **N**ame **L**abels **R**ight and press **Enter**.

   Now the macro is named (\e) and can be run. But first, we need to document the macro.

6. To document the macro, move the cell pointer to cell AC3 (the first cell in the DESCRIPTION column).

7. Type **Macro to erase data at current cell location** and press **Enter**.

Figure 3.1 shows the completed macro.

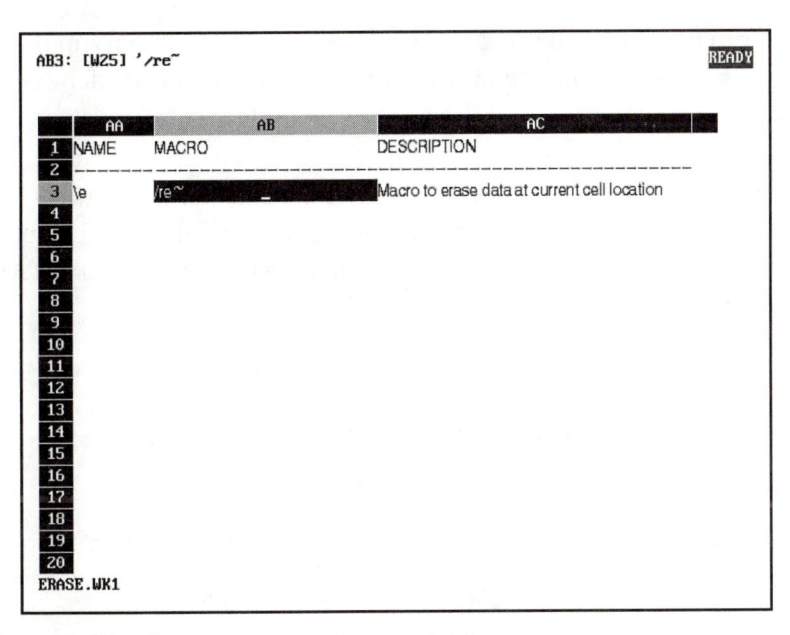

```
AB3: [W25] '/re~                                                    READY

            AA              AB                      AC
    1  NAME           MACRO               DESCRIPTION
    2  ----------------------------------------------------------------
    3  \e             /re~                Macro to erase data at current cell location
    4
    5
    6
    7
    8
    9
   10
   11
   12
   13
   14
   15
   16
   17
   18
   19
   20
   ERASE.WK1
```

Fig. 3.1 The macro to erase the current cell.

25

Easy 1-2-3 Macros

Before we run the macro, we must enter some data to erase. Move the cell pointer to cell A1 and enter your initials. Figure 3.2 shows my initials entered in cell A1.

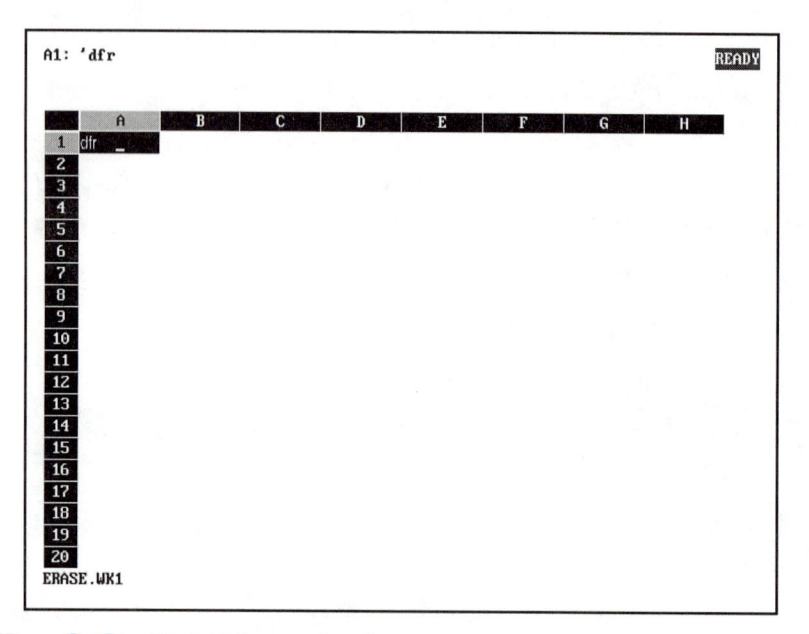

Fig. 3.2 The initials d f r in cell A1.

Let's run the macro. Because this macro is named \e, we can run the macro by pressing and holding the **Alt** key while pressing the letter **E**.

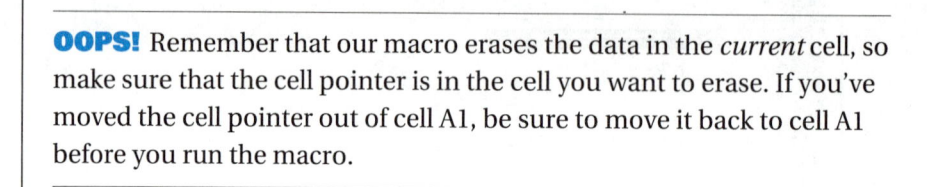

OOPS! Remember that our macro erases the data in the *current* cell, so make sure that the cell pointer is in the cell you want to erase. If you've moved the cell pointer out of cell A1, be sure to move it back to cell A1 before you run the macro.

To run the macro so that it erases the current cell, follow these steps:

1. Move the cell pointer to the cell you want to erase.

   In this example, press the **Home** key to move to cell A1.

2. Press and hold the **Alt** key while you press the letter **E**.

Figure 3.3 shows the initials erased from cell A1.

Writing One-Line Macros That Erase Data

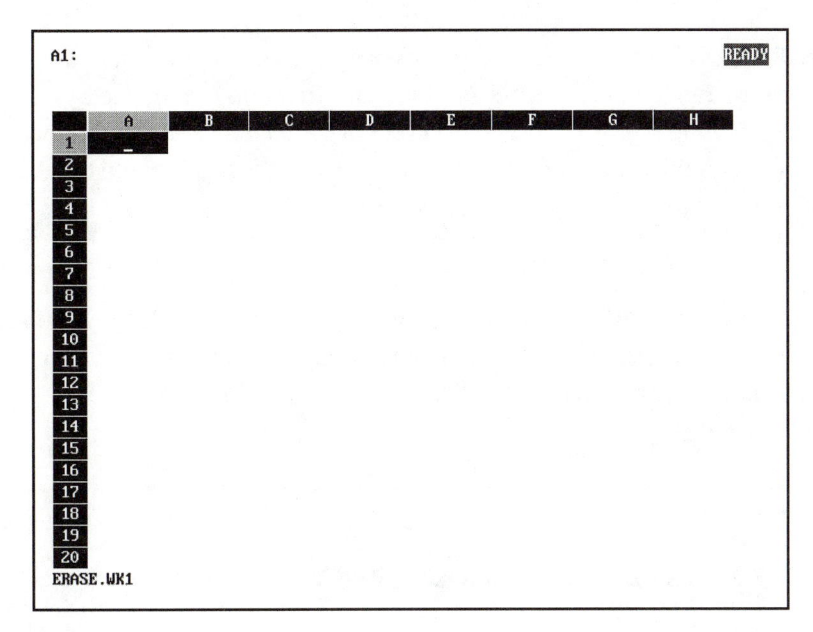

Fig. 3.3 The initials d f r erased from cell A1.

Very good! Next, we'll write a macro to erase data from a group of cells.

A Macro That Erases a Range of Data

Sometimes you need to erase a group of cells rather than a single cell. A group of cells in 1-2-3 is called a *range*. A range is identified in 1-2-3 by indicating the first cell address, followed by two periods, and then the last cell address. To tell 1-2-3 that you want to erase the range of cells A1, A2, A3, B1, B2, B3, C1, C2, and C3, for example, you type A1..C3 at the Enter range to erase: prompt. The two periods mean *include every cell between the two cells provided.* You can type the column letter in the cell address in uppercase or lowercase: A1..C3 is the same as a1..c3.

Suppose that we need a worksheet to track the quarterly income by region for *Josh's Jumping Beans*. Figure 3.4 shows an example of this worksheet. The worksheet has the quarterly income values entered for each region. We're going to write a macro that erases these values. This macro is very useful because it erases all quarterly data in one step; you can use a macro like this from year to year to erase old data and still keep the quarterly/region layout for the data.

Easy 1-2-3 Macros

OOPS! It's always a good idea to save a backup of a file when you plan to erase a range of cells. You can create another copy of the file by using a different file name, such as INCOMES.WKI. Then, if something goes wrong with the erasure, you still have a copy of the original file that you can retrieve and start over with.

Retrieve the file LAYOUT, create the worksheet shown in figure 3.4, and save the worksheet with the name INCOME. The totals in row 12 are @SUM functions. Cell B12, for example, contains the formula `@SUM(B7..B10)`.

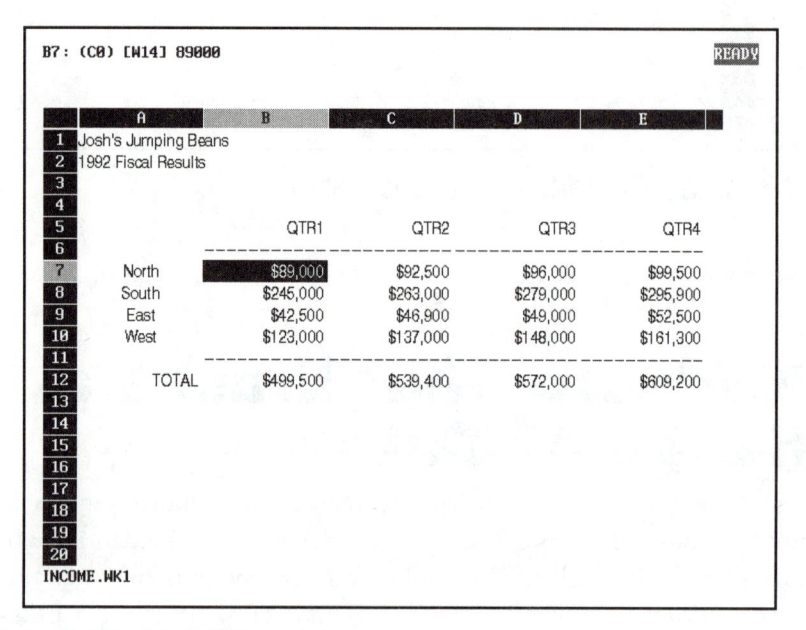

Fig. 3.4 The INCOME worksheet.

Now it's time to write the macro to erase the data in the range B7..E10, the cells that contain the quarterly income values.

1. Move the cell pointer to cell AB3 (the first cell in the MACRO column).

2. Type **'/reB7..E10~** (don't forget the apostrophe!) and press **Enter**.

   /reB7.E10 are the macro instructions to erase the data in cells B7..E10.

3. To name the macro, move the cell pointer to cell AA3 (the first cell in the NAME column).

28

Writing One-Line Macros That Erase Data

4. Type **'\q** and press **Enter**.

   Because this macro erases the quarterly data from this worksheet, we will name it \q (for *quarterly*).

5. Select **/R**ange **N**ame **L**abels **R**ight and press **Enter**.

   Now the macro is named (\q) and can be run. But first, we need to document the macro.

6. To document the macro, move the cell pointer to cell AC3 (the first cell in the DESCRIPTION column).

7. Type **Macro to erase data in cells B7..E10** and press **Enter**.

Figure 3.5 shows the completed macro.

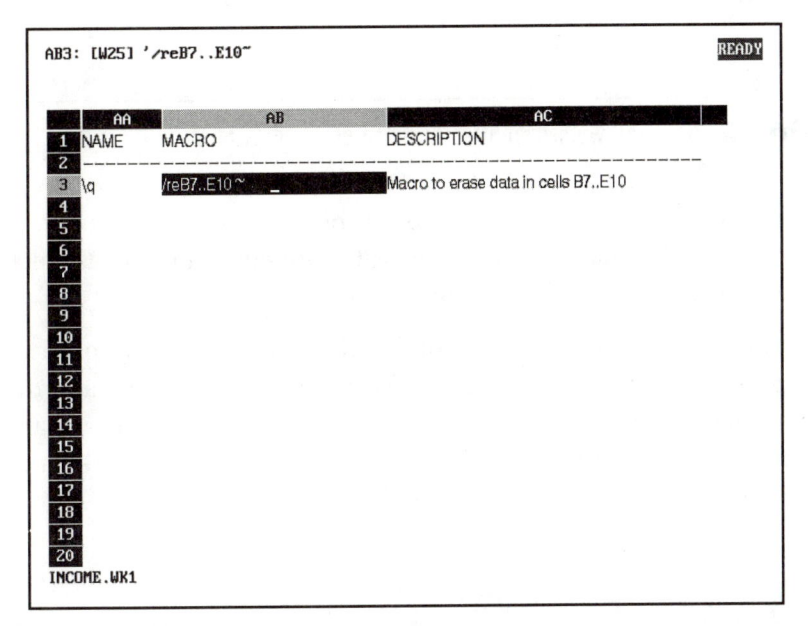

Fig. 3.5 The macro to erase data in the range B7..E10.

Now we're ready to run the macro. Press the **Home** key to move to cell A1 so that you can see the macro perform. Because this macro is named \q, we can run the macro by pressing and holding the **Alt** key while pressing the letter **Q**. Go ahead and run the macro by pressing **Alt**-Q. Figure 3.6 shows that data in the range B7..E10 has been erased after macro \q runs.

29

Easy 1-2-3 Macros

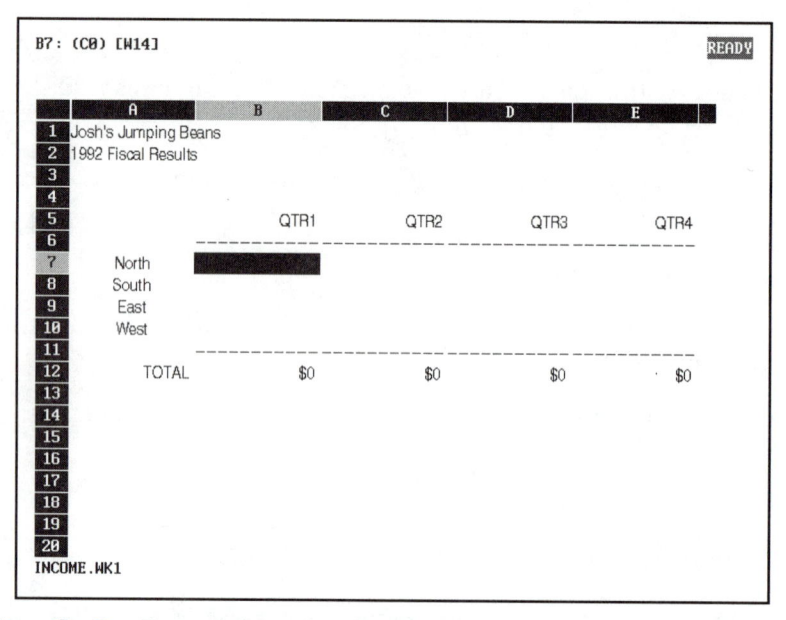

```
B7: (C0) [W14]                                          READY

       A          B         C          D         E
 1  Josh's Jumping Beans
 2  1992 Fiscal Results
 3
 4
 5                QTR1      QTR2       QTR3      QTR4
 6            ---------------------------------------
 7  North
 8  South
 9  East
10  West
11            ---------------------------------------
12     TOTAL      $0        $0         $0        $0
13
14
15
16
17
18
19
20
INCOME.WK1
```

Fig. 3.6   The worksheet after macro \q erases data in range B7..E10.

Note that the formulas in row 12 now display $0. All blank cells have a numerical value of 0. Therefore, the @SUM functions in row 12, which now total blank cells, each calculate to $0.

Nice job! Now we have created and run two different macros to erase data—one that erases data in a single cell and a second that erases data in a range of cells. Each macro performs a /Range Erase operation and can be run quickly by pressing the Alt-*letter* key combination assigned to the macro.

From Here...

You wrote two macros in this chapter. The first macro erased data from a single cell, and the second macro erased data from a range of cells. Erasing data is a common 1-2-3 task, and creating a macro to perform this operation will save you plenty of time and energy.

The macros you create in the next chapter perform column-width operations. We'll create a macro to change the width of a single column, a macro to change the width of several columns, and a macro to change the width of every worksheet column. Now we're cooking!

Creating Simple Macros That Change Column Widths

CHAPTER 4

Easy 1-2-3 Macros

> **NOTE**
>
> If you have the Wysiwyg (What you see is what you get) add-in attached, you don't have an exact correspondence of character-to-column width. All ver-sions of 1-2-3 (except 2.01 and 2.2) have the Wysiwyg add-in. Wysiwyg offers advanced text capabilities and depending on the font, font size, and attribute, you get a different number of characters that fit in a cell.

> **NOTE**
>
> You cannot change the width of an individual cell. You must change the width of an entire column, which changes all cells in that column to the new width.

Changing the width of a column is another task frequently performed in 1-2-3. Every column in a 1-2-3 worksheet has an initial width of 9; this is called the *default column width* and means that an entry in any cell in that column must be nine characters or less to fit properly. A character is any letter, number, or special character, such as the pound sign (#). Often, a width of 9 isn't wide enough for the information in the column. By increasing the column width, you ensure that all information in that column appears on-screen. You can change the width of any column. A column width can be as narrow as 1 or as wide as 240, but usually the width of a column is somewhere between 3 and 45. We're going to write three simple macros in this chapter to change column widths.

A Macro That Changes the Width of a Single Column

A macro to change the width of a column is very useful when you enter names into your worksheet. The name *Kathleen Roche*, for example, needs a column width of 15 (14 characters in the name, plus a space at the end of the name) to fit properly in a cell. The default column width of 9 isn't wide enough. A macro that changes a column width to 25, just in case you get a name like *Robert Horatio Gallagher*, should be part of any worksheet that includes a column of names. The first macro we will write in this chapter changes the column width of a single column.

First, let's identify the *manual* steps necessary to change the column width of a single column:

1. Press **/** to bring up the 1-2-3 main menu.
2. Select **W**orksheet.
3. Select **C**olumn.
4. Select **S**et-Width.
5. Type the number for the column width.
6. Press **Enter**.

The preceding are the steps we need to tell the macro to perform.

In Chapter 2, we built the standard macro layout and saved it with the file name LAYOUT. Let's retrieve the LAYOUT worksheet now so that

Creating Simple Macros That Change Column Widths

we don't have to build the layout again for this macro. Save the file with the name WIDTH so we can use LAYOUT later.

Now you're ready to write the macro. You will write a macro to change a column width to 25.

To create the macro that changes the width of a single column to 25, follow these steps:

1. Move the cell pointer to cell AB3.

2. Type **'/wcs25~** and press **Enter**.

   /wcs25~ are the macro instructions to change the width of the current column to 25.

3. To name the macro, move the cell pointer to cell AA3.

4. Type **'\w** and press **Enter**.

   Because this macro changes the width of a column, we name it \w (for *width*).

5. Select **/R**ange **N**ame **L**abels **R**ight and press **Enter**.

6. To document the macro, move the cell pointer to cell AC3.

7. Type **Macro to change the column width to 25** and press **Enter**.

Figure 4.1 shows the completed macro.

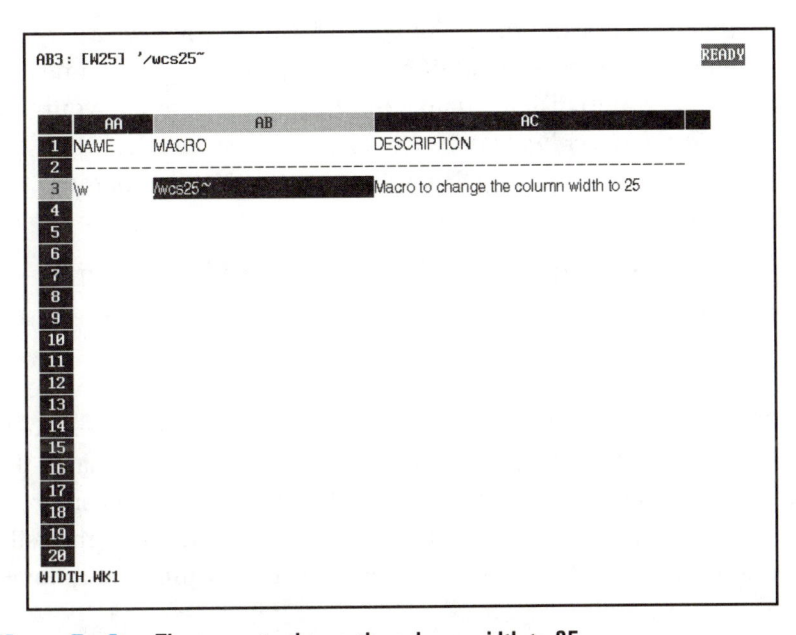

```
AB3: [W25] '/wcs25~                                    READY

         AA          AB                    AC
  1    NAME        MACRO              DESCRIPTION
  2    ----------------------------------------------
  3    \w          /wcs25~            Macro to change the column width to 25
  4
  5
  6
  7
  8
  9
 10
 11
 12
 13
 14
 15
 16
 17
 18
 19
 20
WIDTH.WK1
```

Fig. 4.1 The macro to change the column width to 25.

Easy 1-2-3 Macros

The macro is now complete. Before we run the macro, let's enter some data. Move the cell pointer to cell A1 and enter your full name (I will enter **Donald F. Roche Jr.** for my name). Then move the cell pointer to cell B1 and enter the city or town you live in I will enter **Austin** for my city. Figure 4.2 shows my name in cell A1 and the city Austin in cell B1.

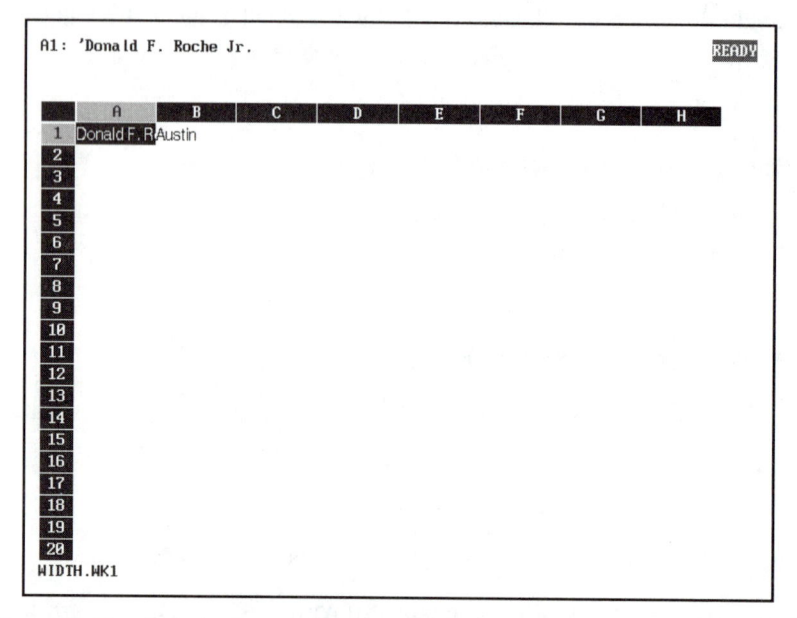

```
A1: 'Donald F. Roche Jr.                                    READY

       A         B       C       D       E       F       G       H
  1  Donald F. R Austin
  2
  3
  4
  5
  6
  7
  8
  9
 10
 11
 12
 13
 14
 15
 16
 17
 18
 19
 20
WIDTH.WK1
```

Fig. 4.2   Data for the macro to widen a single column.

Notice that my name doesn't fit into cell A1. Unless you have a very short name, your name will not fit into cell A1, either. If your name happens to be very short, like the name *Ann Huty*, please pretend your name is *Marilyn-Josephine Bourgesianio* for this lesson—OK, OK, I know that name is kinda long. How about pretending your name is *Sarah Turner*.

Because my name won't fit into cell A1, I need to widen column A. Lucky for me, we just created a macro to accomplish that very task!

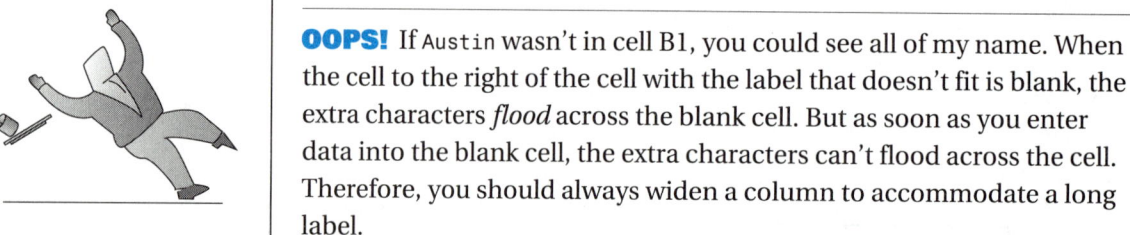

OOPS! If Austin wasn't in cell B1, you could see all of my name. When the cell to the right of the cell with the label that doesn't fit is blank, the extra characters *flood* across the blank cell. But as soon as you enter data into the blank cell, the extra characters can't flood across the cell. Therefore, you should always widen a column to accommodate a long label.

Creating Simple Macros That Change Column Widths

Let's run the macro. Remember that our macro widens a single column—the column containing the cell pointer. Be sure to move the cell pointer back to cell A1 (or any other cell in column A) before you run the macro because we want to widen column A.

Because this macro is named \w, we can run the macro by pressing and holding the **Alt** key while pressing the letter **W**. Go ahead and run the macro by pressing **Alt-W**. Figure 4.3 shows the results of running the \w macro. Notice the [W25] (preceding my name) in the console (upper left portion of the screen). That indicates a width of 25 for the cell. When the cell pointer is at any cell in column A, the [W25] appears in the console because column A has a width of 25.

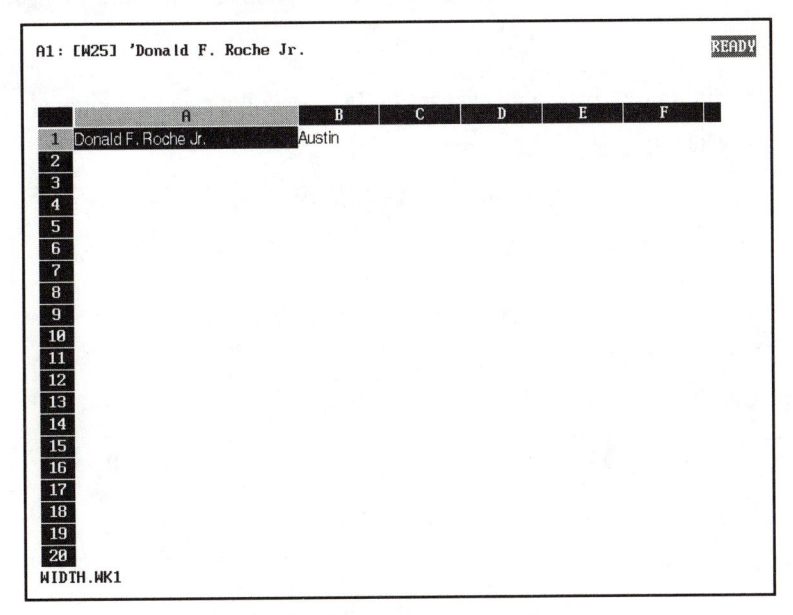

Fig. 4.3 The macro widened column A to 25.

Great! Now you have a macro to widen any worksheet column to 25. You can easily modify this macro to change a column width to 15, 30, 45, or any width you need. Simply change the 25 to the desired width, and you're all set. Next we'll write a macro to widen several columns.

A Macro That Changes the Width of Multiple Columns

> **NOTE**
>
> 1-2-3 Release 2.01 doesn't have the capability to widen multiple columns with one command.

Sometimes you need to widen many columns at once. Suppose that you're entering data for a small worksheet. Each column will contain information that is going to be longer than the default column width of 9. In this case, you need to widen multiple columns at the same time. Granted, you could widen each column individually, but there is no reason to do all that work when you can widen multiple columns with one command. The steps for widening several columns at once are a bit different than the steps for widening a single column.

Let's identify the *manual* steps necessary to change the column widths of multiple columns:

1. Press **/** to bring up the 1-2-3 main menu.
2. Select **W**orksheet.
3. Select **C**olumn.
4. Select **C**olumn-Range.
5. Select **S**et-Width.
6. Specify the columns with the widths you want to change.
7. Type the number for the column width.
8. Press **Enter**.

The worksheet in figure 4.4 contains the column headings NAME, ADDRESS, CITY/STATE/ZIP, and TEL #. The first record for this worksheet is entered and as you can see, we need to adjust the column widths. The information in each of these columns is wider than the default column width of 9, so we must adjust all four column widths.

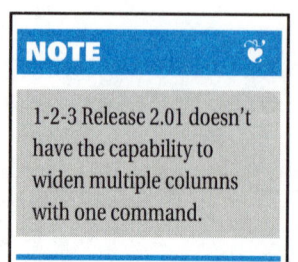

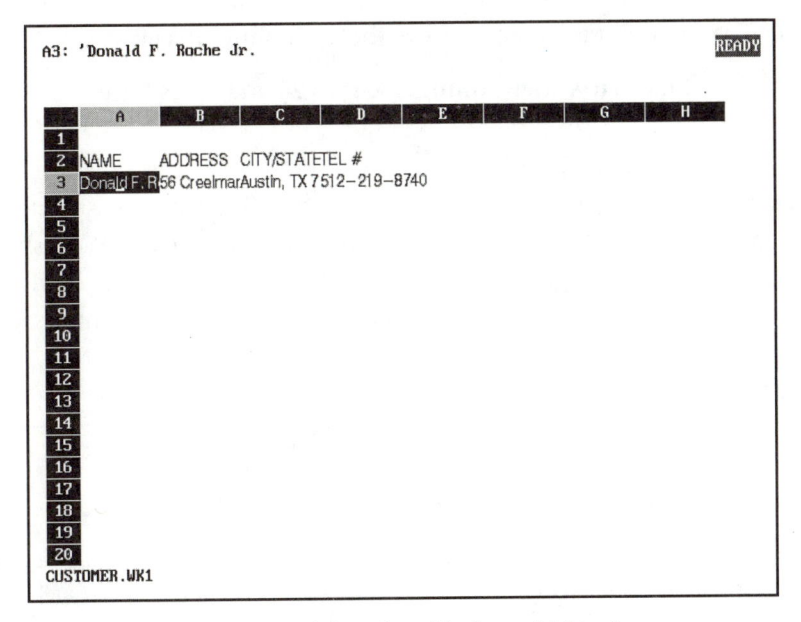

Creating Simple Macros That Change Column Widths

Fig. 4.4 The example worksheet for widening multiple columns.

Retrieve the file LAYOUT and create the worksheet shown in figure 4.4. Type the column headings and enter the information for the first record. Enter your name, address, city, state, ZIP code, and telephone number. Your worksheet should look similar to figure 4.4. Then, save the file with the name CUSTOMER.

Now it's time to write the macro to change the column widths of columns A through D. We will change the column widths of these four columns to 20.

To create the macro that changes the width of multiple columns to 20, follow these steps:

1. Move the cell pointer to cell AB3.

2. Type **'/wccsA1..D1~20~** and press **Enter**.

   /wccsA1 are the macro instructions to change the column widths of columns A through D to 20.

3. To name the macro, move the cell pointer to cell AA3.

4. Type **'\s** and press **Enter**.

   Because this macro widens several columns, we name it \s (for *several*).

5. Select **/R**ange **N**ame **L**abels **R**ight and press **Enter**.

Easy 1-2-3 Macros

6. To document the macro, move the cell pointer to cell AC3.

7. Type **Macro to widen columns A-D to 20** and press **Enter**.

OOPS! When you change the widths of several columns, you select the columns whose widths you want to change (after you select **/W**orksheet **C**olumn **C**olumn **R**ange). Then you select the width. For example, if you want to change the column widths of columns A-M to 20, the macro is /wccs A1..M1~20~. First the columns change and then the width changes.

Figure 4.5 shows the completed macro.

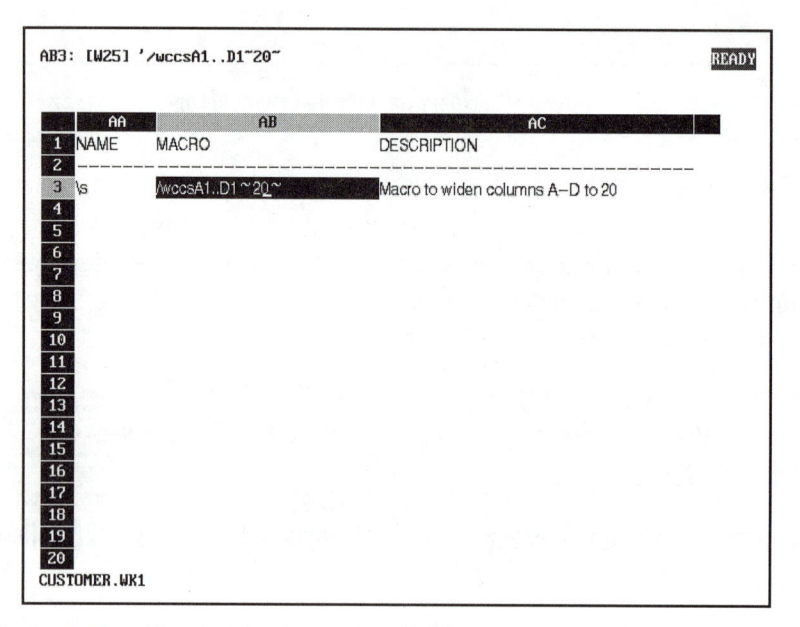

```
AB3: [W25] '/wccsA1..D1~20~                                    READY

           AA            AB                    AC
   1   NAME          MACRO               DESCRIPTION
   2   ─────────────────────────────────────────────────
   3   \s            /wccsA1..D1~20~     Macro to widen columns A-D to 20
   4
   5
   6
   7
   8
   9
  10
  11
  12
  13
  14
  15
  16
  17
  18
  19
  20
CUSTOMER.WK1
```

Fig. 4.5 The macro to change the widths of columns A through D to 20.

Now we're ready to run the macro. Press the **Home** key to move the cell pointer to cell A1 so that you can see the macro perform. Because this macro is named \s, we can run the macro by pressing **Alt-S**. Go ahead and run the macro. Figure 4.6 shows the worksheet after macro \s has been run; columns A through D are widened to 20.

Creating Simple Macros That Change Column Widths

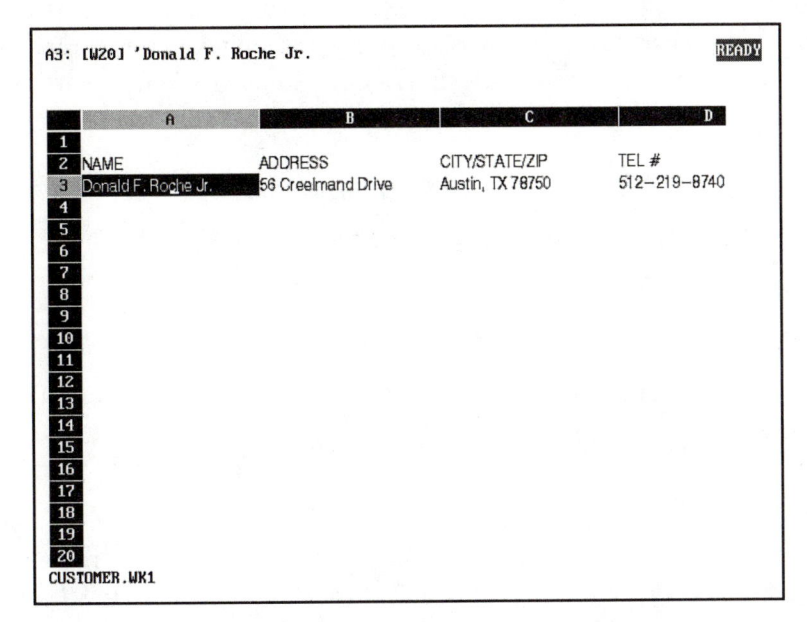

```
A3: [W20] 'Donald F. Roche Jr.                                    READY

           A                  B              C              D
   1
   2  NAME              ADDRESS         CITY/STATE/ZIP   TEL #
   3  Donald F. Roche Jr. 56 Creelmand Drive Austin, TX 78750  512-219-8740
   4
   5
   6
   7
   8
   9
  10
  11
  12
  13
  14
  15
  16
  17
  18
  19
  20
CUSTOMER.WK1
```

Fig. 4.6   The worksheet after columns A through D are widened to 20.

Notice the [W20] in the console with the cell pointer in cell A3. Because column A is now a width of 20, as are columns B, C, and D, all cells in each of those columns will display [W20] when the cell pointer is in a cell in one of those columns.

A Macro That Changes the Width of All Columns

You also can change the width of every column in the worksheet with one command. As mentioned earlier, every column in a worksheet has an initial width of 9, which is the default column width. You can change the default column width, however, and that changes the width of every column. If you change the default column width to 15, every column in the worksheet will have a width of 15.

I often change my default column width to 15 when I'm creating a worksheet for a client who reports annual company revenues in the millions. If I format the value cells to Currency with 2 Decimal Places, the cells containing those values must be at least a width of 11 for a value in the millions to display. I make the width 15 to give myself some elbow room; I hate crowded worksheets!

39

Easy 1-2-3 Macros

To change all column widths, you execute a default column-width change. As always, let's identify the *manual* steps for our macro to perform.

The steps for widening all the worksheet columns follow:

1. Press **/** to bring up the 1-2-3 main menu.
2. Select **W**orksheet.
3. Select **G**lobal.
4. Select **C**olumn-Width.
5. Type the number for the default column width.
6. Press **Enter**.

Once again, retrieve the file LAYOUT. Now we'll write the macro to change all the columns in a worksheet to a width of 15. Save the file with the name EVERYONE.

To create the macro that changes all column widths of a worksheet to 15, follow these steps:

1. Move the cell pointer to cell AB3.
2. Type **'/wgc15~** and press **Enter**.

    /wgc15~ are the macro instructions to change all columns in the worksheet to a width of 15.

3. To name the macro, move the cell pointer to cell AA3.
4. Type **'\a** and press **Enter**.

    Because this is a macro to change all column widths to 15, we will name it \a (for *all*).

5. Select **/R**ange **N**ame **L**abels **R**ight and press **Enter**.
6. To document the macro, move the cell pointer to cell AC3.
7. Type **Macro to change the default column width to 15** and press **Enter**.

Figure 4.7 shows the completed macro.

40

Creating Simple Macros That Change Column Widths

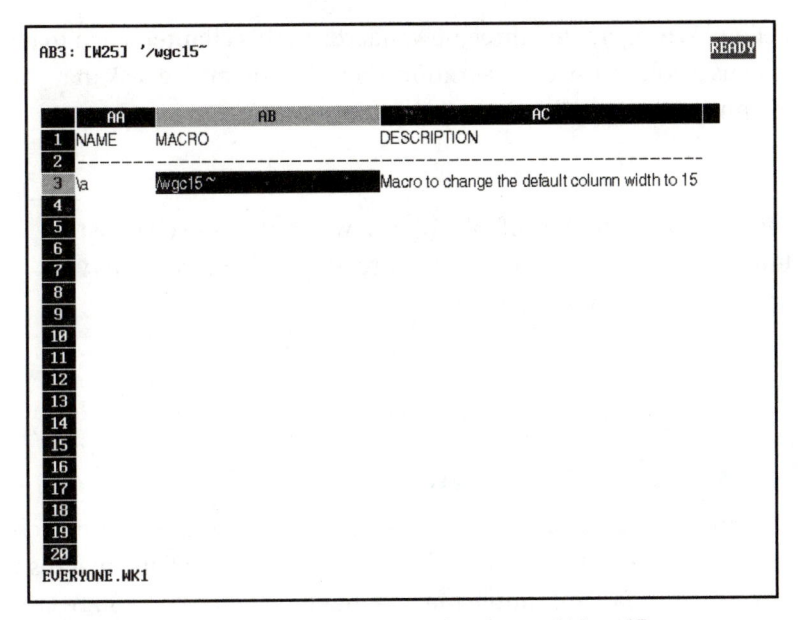

Fig. 4.7 The macro to change the default column width to 15.

Now we're ready to run the macro. Because this macro is named \a, we can run the macro by pressing Alt-A. Go ahead and run the macro. Figure 4.8 shows the worksheet after macro \a runs; all the columns now have a width of 15.

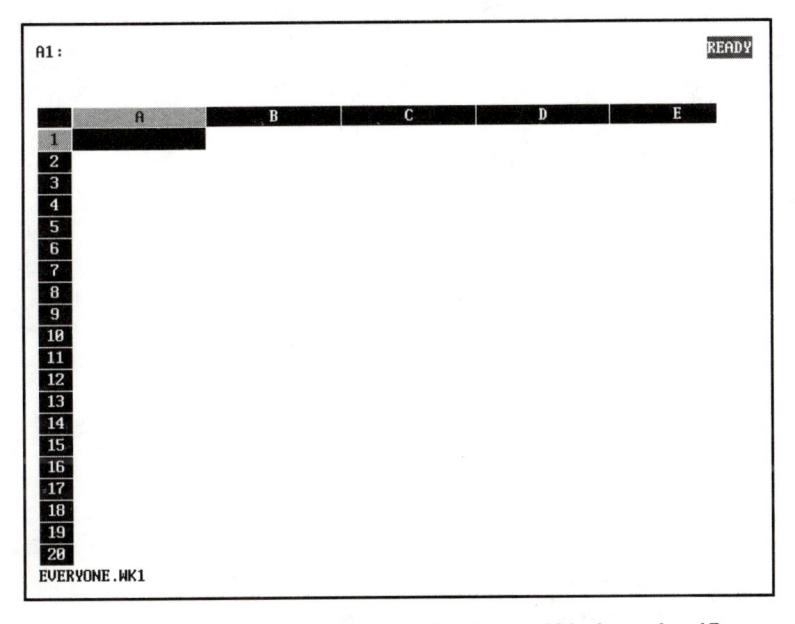

Fig. 4.8 The worksheet with the default column width changed to 15.

Excellent! We've created three new macros in this chapter. Each macro performs a column-width operation—another repetitive task that you now can quickly handle with a macro.

OOPS! A change to the default column width *does not* change the column width of any column width already changed with the /wcs command or the /wccs command.

From Here...

In this chapter, we wrote macros to widen a single column, several columns, and all worksheet columns. These macros, like all the macros we have created so far, are simple macros that help you when you're creating and working with a worksheet.

The macros we create in the next chapter perform number-formatting operations. We'll create three macros that each assign different numeric formats.

Creating Simple Macros That Format Numbers

CHAPTER

5

Easy 1-2-3 Macros

After you enter values into your worksheet, you often want to format the values to look a certain way. If you're creating a financial worksheet, for example, you often want the numbers to appear in a Currency format. If you're creating a worksheet to show percentages, you want the numbers to appear as a Percent format. Formatting numbers is certainly a task you'll do many times. Writing macros that format numbers can save you a tremendous amount of time. We're going to create three simple macros in this chapter to format numbers.

A Macro That Formats a Range as Comma with 2 Decimal Places

A cell or range of cells can be given a name, called a *range name*. For example, you can give the name BUDGET to cells A5..C15. Then when you want to affect cells A5..C15, you can use the name BUDGET. For example, the macro /reBUDGET~ would erase cells A5..C15. The advantage of using range names is that range names adjust if the structure of your worksheet changes. Also, a name is easier to remember than a cell address. The first macro we write in this chapter will change the format of a range of cells to Comma with 2 Decimal Places.

Let's identify the *manual* steps necessary to change a range of cells to Comma with 2 Decimal Places:

1. Press **/** to bring up the main 1-2-3 menu.
2. Select **R**ange.
3. Select **F**ormat.
4. Select **,** (the choice for comma is not the word *comma*, but the comma itself).
5. Press **Enter** to accept the default of 2 decimal places.
6. Specify the range of cells to format.
7. Press **Enter**.

The preceding steps are the steps we need to tell the macro to perform.

Retrieve the LAYOUT worksheet and save it with the name FORMAT. We'll write the macro in the FORMAT file. Figure 5.1 shows a worksheet

Creating Simple Macros That Format Numbers

with a range of numbers currently unformatted. The range of unformatted cells is B6..E11. The numbers in row 11 are calculated numbers using the @SUM function. Create the worksheet shown in figure 5.1.

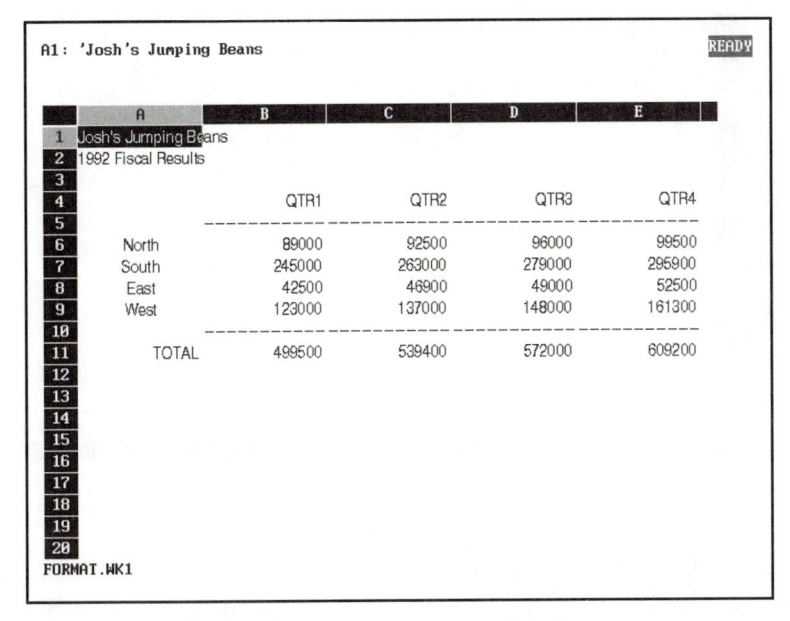

Fig. 5.1 The FORMAT worksheet with unformatted numbers.

We will write a macro to change the format of the range B6..E11 to Comma with 2 Decimal Places. To create this macro, follow these steps:

1. Move the cell pointer to cell AB3.

2. Type **'/rf,~B6..E11~** and press **Enter**.

   /rf,~B6..E11 are the macro instructions to change the format of cells B6..E11 to Comma with 2 Decimal Places.

3. To name the macro, move the cell pointer to cell AA3.

4. Type **'\c** press **Enter**.

   Because this is a macro to format cells to Comma with 2 Decimal Places, we will name it \c (for *comma*).

5. Select **/R**ange **N**ame **L**abels **R**ight and press **Enter**.

6. To document the macro, move the cell pointer to cell AC3.

7. Type **Macro to change format of B6..E11 to (,2)** and press **Enter**.

Figure 5.2 shows the completed macro.

Easy 1-2-3 Macros

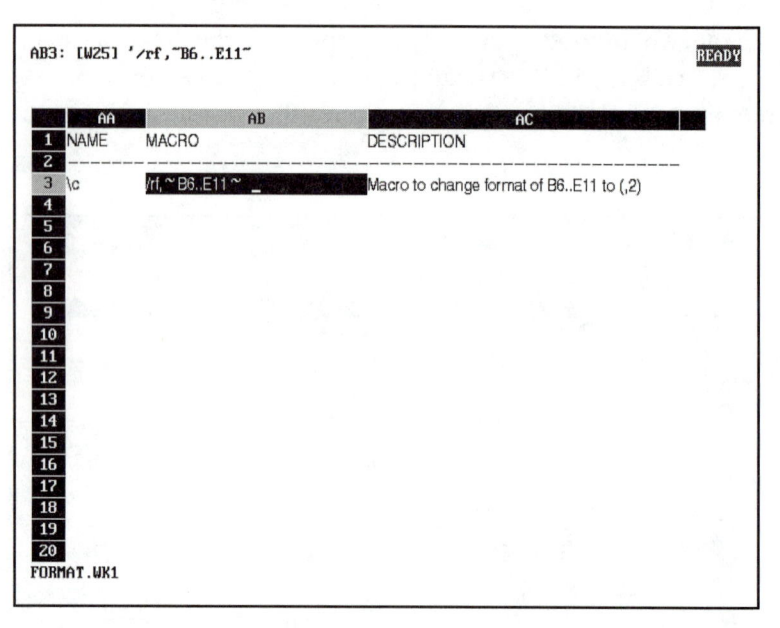

Fig. 5.2 The macro to change the format of the range B6..E11 to Comma with 2 Decimal Places.

Let's run the macro. Move the cell pointer to cell B6 so that we can watch the macro perform. Because this macro is named \c, we can run the macro by pressing **Alt-C**. Go ahead and run the macro. Figure 5.3 shows the results of running the \c macro.

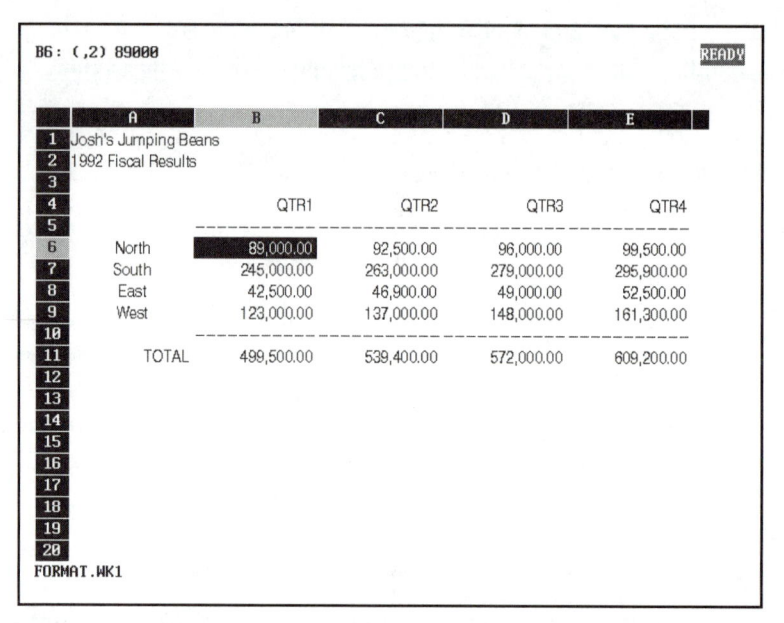

Fig. 5.3 The range B6..E11 formatted as Comma with 2 Decimal Places.

46

Creating Simple Macros That Format Numbers

Good job! Now you have created a macro to format a range of cells to Comma with 2 Decimal Places. Next, we'll write a macro to format a range of cells to Currency with 0 Decimal Places.

A Macro That Formats a Range as Currency with 0 Decimal Places

1-2-3 has many value formats. The Currency format is perhaps the most frequently used. Many times the values in a worksheet are currency figures, and you want them to appear with a dollar sign. The steps for formatting a range of cells as Currency with 0 Decimal Places are very similar to the steps for formatting a range of cells as Comma with 2 Decimal Places.

Let's identify the *manual* steps for setting a Currency with 0 Decimal Places format:

1. Press **/** to bring up the main 1-2-3 menu.
2. Select **R**ange.
3. Select **F**ormat.
4. Select **C**urrency.
5. Press **0** (zero) for zero decimal places.
6. Press **Enter**.
7. Specify the range of cells to format.
8. Press **Enter**.

Retrieve the FORMAT worksheet, which is the file we created in the last section. Let's write the macro to change the format of cells B6..E11 to Currency with 0 Decimal Places.

To create this macro, follow these steps:

1. Move the cell pointer to cell AB3.
2. Type **'/rfc0~B6..E11~** and press **Enter**.

   /rfc0~B6..E11~ are the macro instructions to change the format of range B6..E11 to Currency with 0 Decimal Places.

3. To name the macro, move the cell pointer to cell AA3.

Easy 1-2-3 Macros

4. Type **'\d** and press **Enter**.

   Because this is a macro to format cells to Currency, we will name it \d (for *dollars*).

5. Select **/R**ange **N**ame **L**abels **R**ight and press **Enter**.

6. To document the macro, move the cell pointer to cell AC3.

7. Type **Macro to change format of B6..E11 to (C0)** and press **Enter**.

Figure 5.4 shows the completed macro.

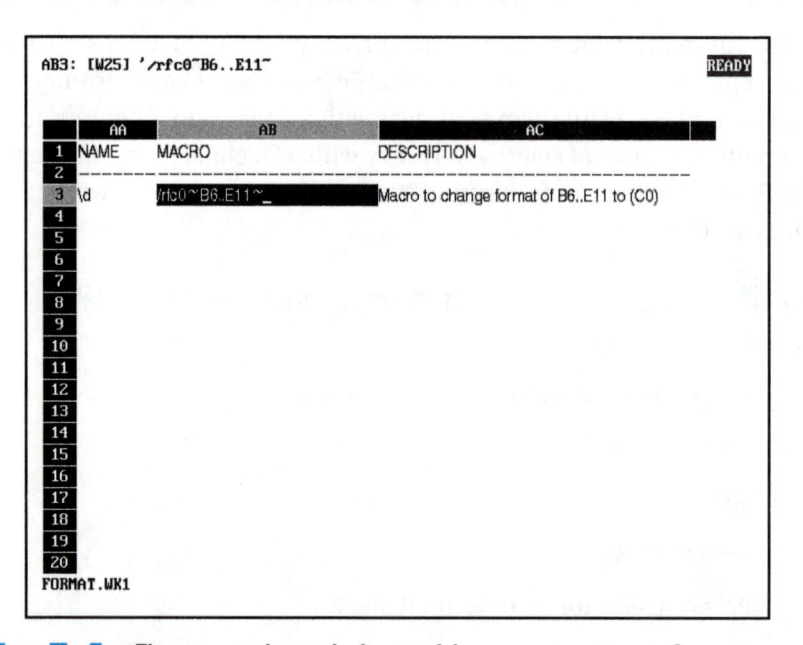

```
AB3: [W25] '/rfc0~B6..E11~                                          READY

         AA           AB                      AC
    1  NAME         MACRO              DESCRIPTION
    2  ---------------------------------------------------------
    3  \d           /rfc0~B6..E11~_    Macro to change format of B6..E11 to (C0)
    4
    5
    6
    7
    8
    9
   10
   11
   12
   13
   14
   15
   16
   17
   18
   19
   20
   FORMAT.WK1
```

Fig. 5.4 The macro to change the format of the range B6..E11 to Currency with 0 Decimal Places.

Let's run the macro. Move the cell pointer to cell B6 so that we can watch the macro perform. Because this macro is named \d, we can run the macro by pressing **Alt**-D. Go ahead and run the macro. Figure 5.5 shows the results of running the \d macro.

Creating Simple Macros That Format Numbers

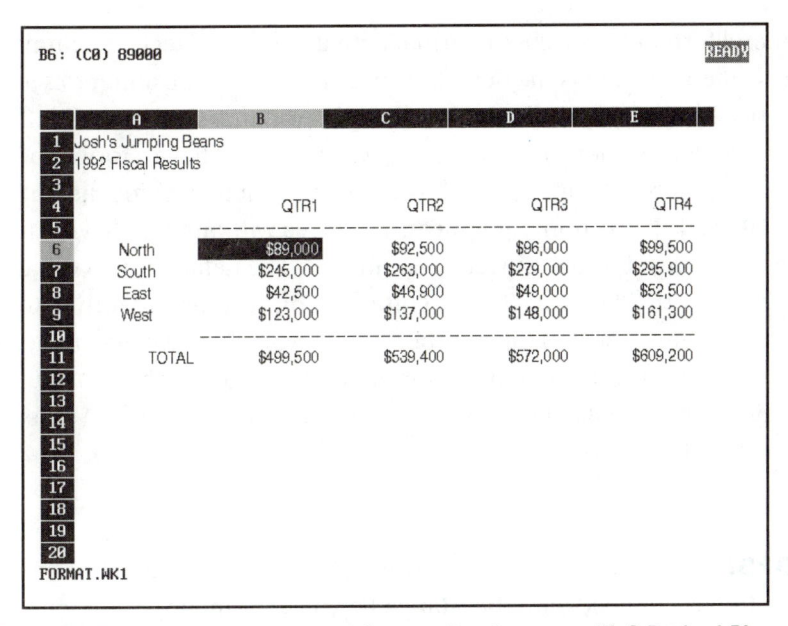

```
B6: (C0) 89000                                              READY

      A           B          C          D          E
 1  Josh's Jumping Beans
 2  1992 Fiscal Results
 3
 4                QTR1       QTR2       QTR3       QTR4
 5              ─────────────────────────────────────────
 6  North        $89,000    $92,500    $96,000    $99,500
 7  South       $245,000   $263,000   $279,000   $295,900
 8  East         $42,500    $46,900    $49,000    $52,500
 9  West        $123,000   $137,000   $148,000   $161,300
10              ─────────────────────────────────────────
11  TOTAL       $499,500   $539,400   $572,000   $609,200
12
...
20
FORMAT.WK1
```

Fig. 5.5 The range B6..E11 formatted as Currency with 0 Decimal Places.

Another macro in the repertoire! Whew! The next macro will change the default cell format to Currency with 2 Decimal Places.

OOPS! If a formatted number cannot be fully displayed in a cell because the cell width is too narrow, asterisks (* * *) appear in the cell. Simply widen the column, and the number displays fully.

A Macro That Changes the Default Cell Format to Currency with 2 Decimal Places

Just as you can change the width of every column in the worksheet with one command, you can change the format of every cell in the worksheet with one command. Every cell in the worksheet, by default, has a

Easy 1-2-3 Macros

General format. The General format actually has no effect on a number. The General format is the default format, and, as we are about to see, can be changed. If you change the default format to Currency with 2 Decimal Places, then *every cell in the worksheet* will have a format of Currency with 2 Decimal Places. That means that if you type the number `10` in a cell, the number appears as `$10.00` without your having to use the /**R**ange **F**ormat **C**urrency command. The default for all values is Currency with 2 Decimal Places. I often change my default format to Currency when most of the numbers in my worksheet will be financial numbers. If I'm going to have to format most of the numbers for Currency, I may as well change the default format to Currency and save myself a lot of time.

OOPS! A change to the default format doesn't change the format of a cell already changed with the /**R**ange **F**ormat command.

To change the format for all cells, you execute a global format change. Let's identify the steps for our macro to perform.

The steps for *manually* formatting all the worksheet cells follow:

1. Press / to bring up the main 1-2-3 menu.
2. Select **W**orksheet.
3. Select **G**lobal.
4. Select **F**ormat.
5. Select **C**urrency.
6. Press **2** for two decimal places.
7. Press **Enter**.

Once again, retrieve the FORMAT worksheet. This time, to better illustrate this macro, we want to erase the numbers in this worksheet. Erase the data in the ranges B6..E9 and B11..E11. We also need to reset the format to General, the current default format. Erasing the data from a cell doesn't eliminate the format. Use the /**R**ange **F**ormat **R**eset command to reset the format of cells B6..E9 and B11..E11. Now we'll write

Creating Simple Macros That Format Numbers

the macro to change the format of all cells to Currency with 2 Decimal Places. Your worksheet should look like figure 5.6.

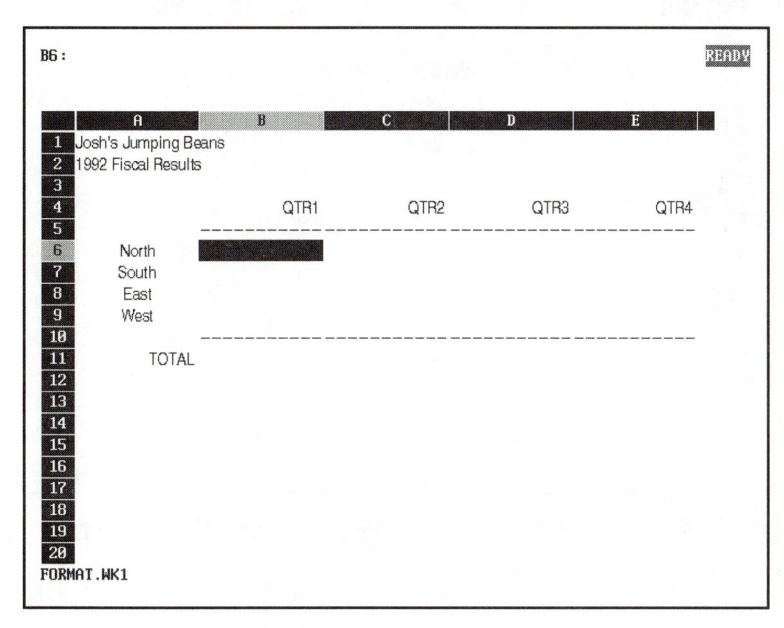

Fig. 5.6 The blank FORMAT worksheet.

To create the macro to change the default cell format, follow these steps:

1. Move the cell pointer to cell AB3.

2. Type **'/wgfc2~** and press **Enter**.

   /wgfc2~ are the macro instructions to change the format of all cells in the worksheet to Currency with 2 Decimal Places.

3. To name the macro, move the cell pointer to cell AA3.

4. Type **'\b** and press **Enter**.

   Because this macro changes the format of all the cells in the worksheet to Currency, we will name it \b (for *big-time buckos*).

5. Select **/R**ange **N**ame **L**abels **R**ight and press **Enter**.

6. To document the macro, move the cell pointer to cell AC3.

7. Type **Macro to change the default format to (C2)** and press **Enter**.

Figure 5.7 shows the completed macro.

Easy 1-2-3 Macros

```
AB3: [W25] '/wgfc2~                                          READY

         AA              AB                    AC
   1  NAME          MACRO              DESCRIPTION
   2  ------------------------------------------------------------
   3  \b            /wgfc2~            Macro to change the default format to (C2)
   4
   5
   6
   7
   8
   9
  10
  11
  12
  13
  14
  15
  16
  17
  18
  19
  20
FORMAT.WK1
```

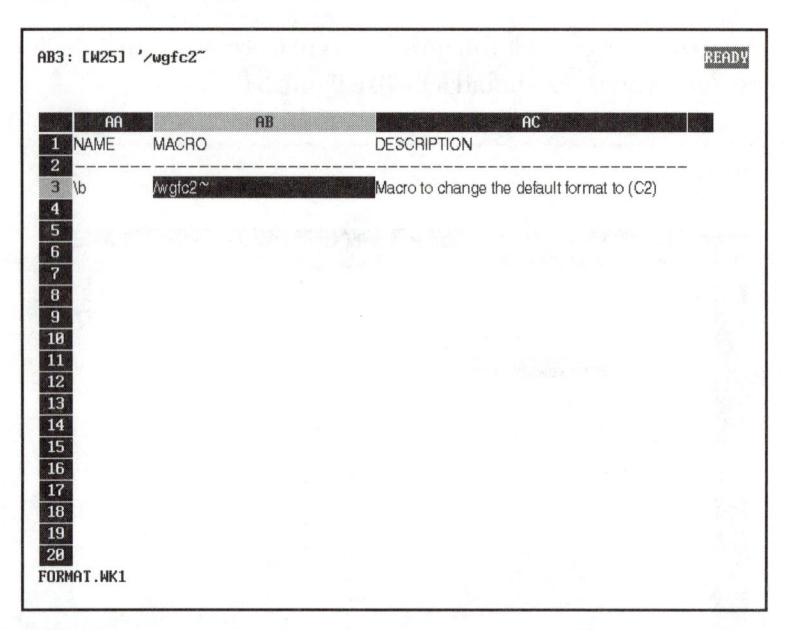

Fig. 5.7 The macro to change the default cell format to Currency with 2 Decimal Places.

Now we're ready to run the macro. Move the cell pointer to cell B6. Because this macro is named \b, we can run the macro by pressing **Alt-B**. Go ahead and run the macro.

Figure 5.8 shows the worksheet after macro \b runs; it looks as though nothing has happened. Type the number **89000** in cell B6 and press **Enter**. Notice that the number automatically appears in the Currency with 2 Decimal Places format!

Creating Simple Macros That Format Numbers

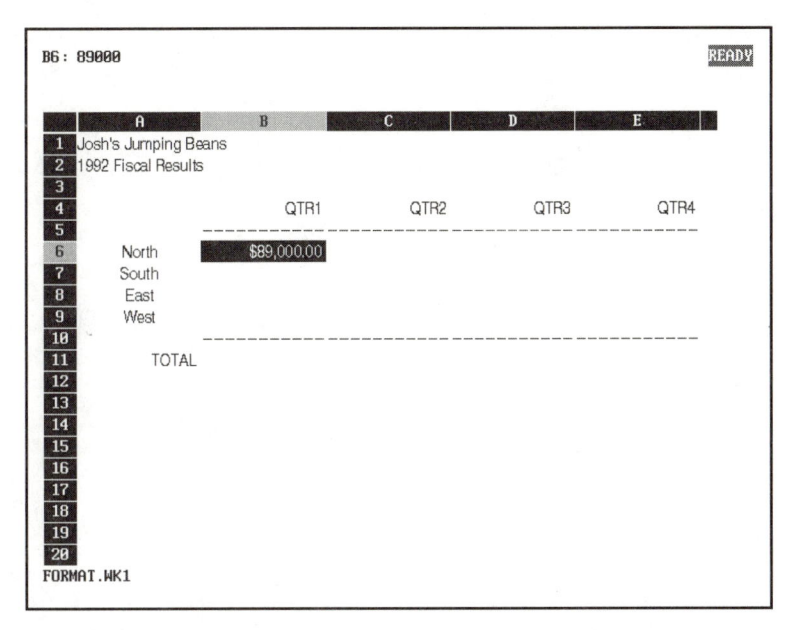

```
B6: 89000                                    READY

       A           B          C          D          E
  1  Josh's Jumping Beans
  2  1992 Fiscal Results
  3
  4               QTR1       QTR2       QTR3       QTR4
  5               ----------------------------------------
  6    North     $89,000.00
  7    South
  8    East
  9    West
 10               ----------------------------------------
 11    TOTAL
 12
 13
 14
 15
 16
 17
 18
 19
 20
FORMAT.WK1
```

Fig. 5.8   The number 8 9 0 0 0 appears automatically with the default format of Currency with 2 Decimal Places.

Excellent! We've created three new macros in this chapter. Each macro changes the format of worksheet values—another repetitive task that you now can handle quickly with a macro.

From Here...

You created three more macros in this chapter, and each macro changed the format of number cells. Formatting is a task you perform often with 1-2-3, and these macros will save you a great deal of time.

The next chapter discusses ways to test macros. We will explore STEP mode, using Undo, and other 1-2-3 capabilities that are available for macro testing.

Testing and Automating Macros

PART II

Testing Macros

CHAPTER 6

Easy 1-2-3 Macros

After you create a macro, you must test it to ensure that it works correctly. Testing macros is a natural part of creating the macro. Sometimes a macro runs correctly the first time you run it, and sometimes it doesn't. If it doesn't run correctly, you need to know how to find the problem and fix it.

You test a macro by saving the file with the name TEST and then by running the macro. If the macro performs the task correctly, you're all set; if it doesn't perform the task correctly, you need to correct the macro. Short macros don't require much effort to test. The macro you created to erase a cell in Chapter 3 was a short, four-keystroke macro. When you run the macro, the contents of the current cell should be erased. If the cell contents aren't erased, you must correct the macro. With only four keystrokes to review and correct, this process isn't too difficult. Complex macros that perform multiple tasks frequently, however, require quite a bit of effort at the testing stage.

1-2-3 comes equipped with a feature that makes correcting macros simple. This feature is called *STEP mode*. STEP mode is a very useful tool for locating problems with your macros. By changing some of the macros you have created and by making them run incorrectly, you can run the macro in STEP mode and find the problem.

Using STEP Mode To Test Macros

1-2-3's STEP mode is ideal for isolating mistakes in a macro. With STEP mode turned on, 1-2-3 executes the macro step-by-step, one instruction at a time. After each instruction, 1-2-3 waits for you to press a key before proceeding to the next instruction. You can press any key, but pressing the space bar is the most convenient.

You turn STEP mode on or off by pressing Alt-F2. STEP mode isn't on when you first load 1-2-3. When you turn STEP mode on by pressing Alt-F2, the STEP indicator appears at the bottom of the screen. When you start the macro you want to test, the STEP indicator disappears and the macro appears in the lower left corner of the screen. If the macro is a multiple-line macro, the first line of the macro appears in the lower left corner of the screen. A rectangle appears on the first command of the macro and moves to each command as you press a key to "step through" the macro; this process enables you to know exactly which command is being executed. The STEP indicator reappears when the macro ends. You turn off STEP mode by pressing Alt-F2 again.

> **NOTE**
>
> Correcting macros is called *debugging* macros. When a macro doesn't run correctly, it's said to have a *bug*.

> **NOTE**
>
> In Release 3.x, a menu appears when you press Alt-F2. Select Step to access STEP mode in these 1-2-3 Releases.

Testing Macros

OOPS! STEP mode doesn't automatically turn off when the macro is done executing. You must turn off STEP mode by pressing **Alt-F2**.

When you invoke a macro to test in Releases 2.01 or 3.x, for example, the STEP indicator changes to a blinking SST indicator. This change tells you that 1-2-3 is waiting for you to press a key before the software executes the first macro instruction. When the macro ends, the SST indicator disappears and the STEP indicator reappears. You then turn STEP mode off by pressing **Alt-F2**. You can stop stepping through a macro by pressing **Ctrl-Break**, which stops the macro.

Stepping through a Macro That Erases Data

You can use STEP mode with any macro, but you normally don't need to with a very short macro. We, however, are going to use the short macros we wrote in Chapters 3 through 5 to learn about STEP mode. Retrieve the INCOME worksheet (see fig. 6.1). The macro in this file erases a range of cells. We're going to modify the macro to include an error and then run the macro in STEP mode to help find the problem.

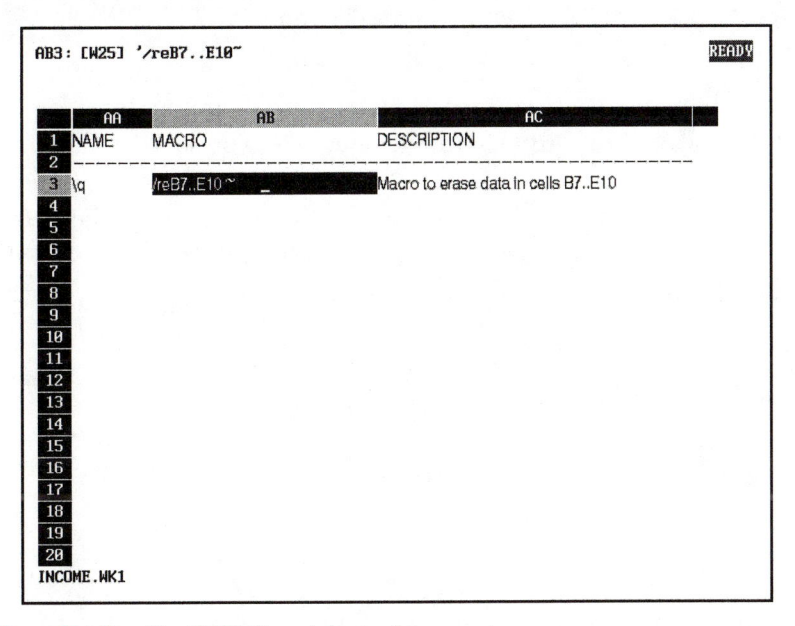

Fig. 6.1 The INCOME worksheet with macro \q.

Easy 1-2-3 Macros

We're going to change the cell address in cell AB3 of the macro from E10 to just E. (A cell consists of a column letter and row number.) Because E is only a column letter, an error occurs when we run the macro. Edit cell AB3 so the macro reads /reB7..E~. Figure 6.2 shows the modified macro.

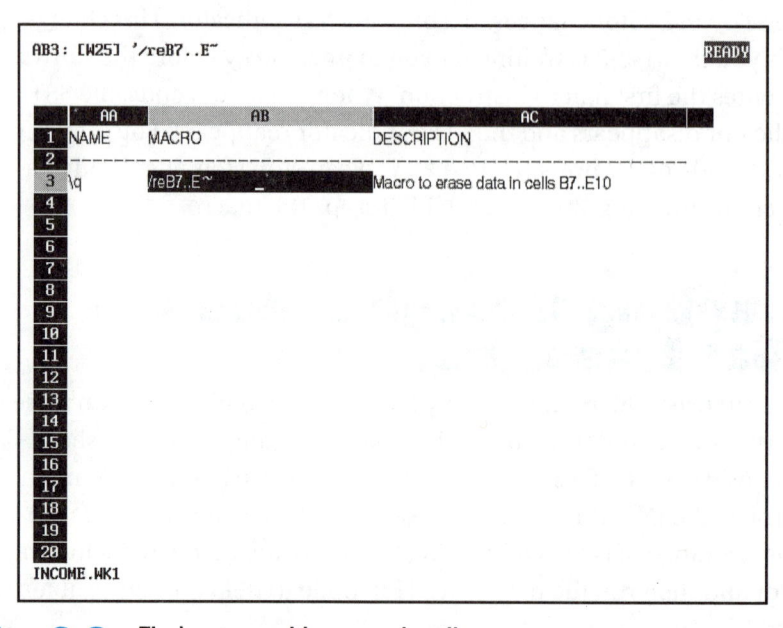

Fig. 6.2 The \q macro with an error in cell AB3.

Now let's run the macro and see what happens. Press the **Home** key to move to cell A1. Press **Alt-Q** to run the macro. As you see, the macro doesn't work correctly. The **/R**ange **E**rase command doesn't execute because the invalid cell address E caused an error. Figure 6.3 shows the error message, which appears in Release 2.3, indicating an invalid cell or range address that appears when the macro runs.

Testing Macros

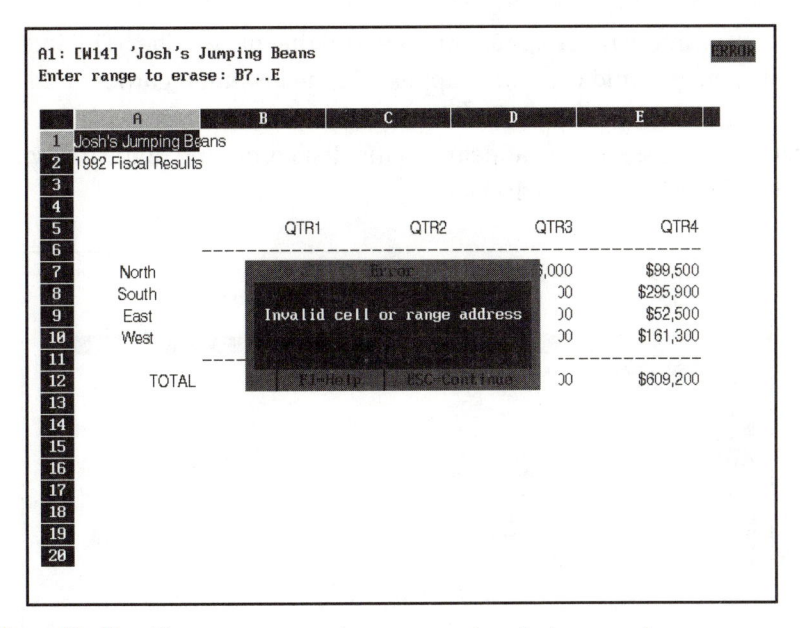

Fig. 6.3 The error message that appears when the \q macro is run.

Let's run the macro with STEP mode turned on and find the problem. First, press **Esc** to remove the error message and return to READY mode. Now turn on STEP mode by pressing **Alt-F2**. The STEP indicator appears at the bottom of the screen (see fig. 6.4).

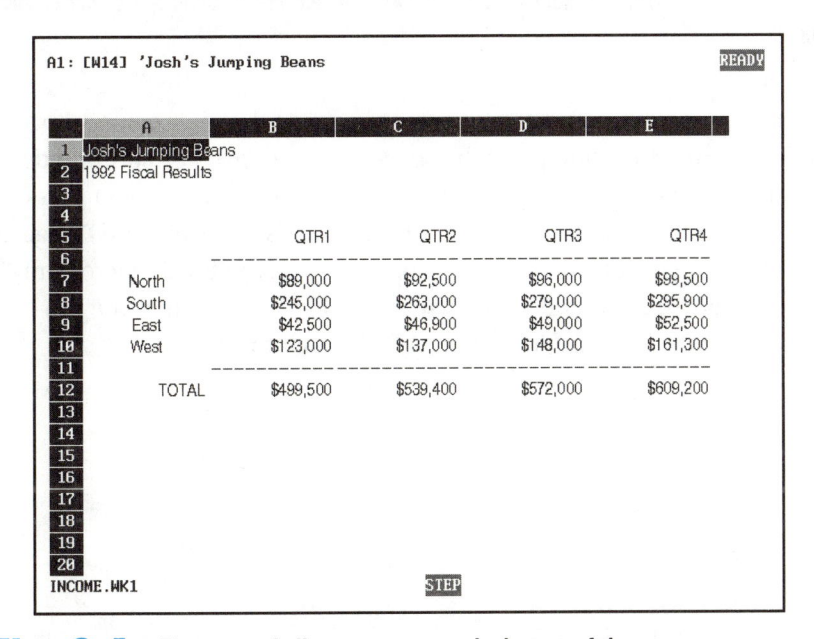

Fig. 6.4 The STEP indicator appears at the bottom of the screen.

Easy 1-2-3 Macros

Next, we run the macro. Press Alt-Q to run the macro. The STEP indicator disappears, and the macro appears in the lower left corner of the screen (see fig. 6.5). The cell address of the macro appears with the macro itself. A rectangle appears on the first command of the macro, which, for this macro, is the slash (/).

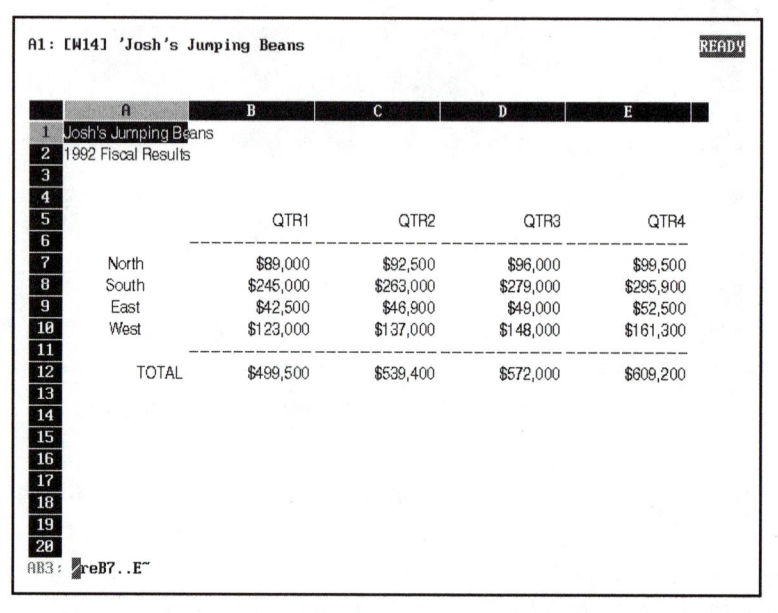

Fig. 6.5 The cell address and the macro appear in the lower left corner of the screen.

Press the space bar, and 1-2-3 begins executing the macro one step at a time. The first time you press the space bar, the slash key command is executed and the 1-2-3 main menu appears. The next time you press the space bar, the second macro command, r, is executed and Range is selected. The next time you press the space bar, the third macro command, e, is executed and Erase is selected. Figure 6.6 shows the progression of the reverse video rectangle through the macro.

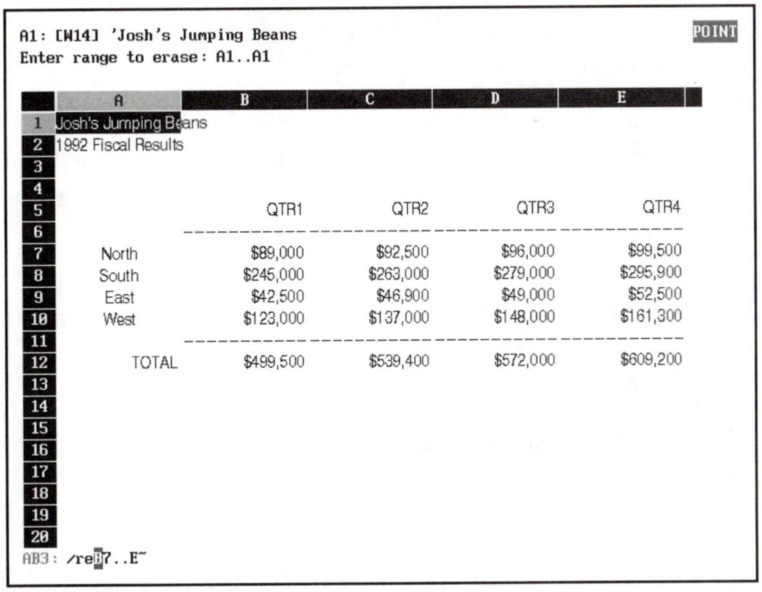

Testing Macros

```
A1: [W14] 'Josh's Jumping Beans                          POINT
Enter range to erase: A1..A1
```

	A	B	C	D	E
1	Josh's Jumping Beans				
2	1992 Fiscal Results				
3					
4					
5		QTR1	QTR2	QTR3	QTR4
6		--------	--------	--------	--------
7	North	$89,000	$92,500	$96,000	$99,500
8	South	$245,000	$263,000	$279,000	$295,900
9	East	$42,500	$46,900	$49,000	$52,500
10	West	$123,000	$137,000	$148,000	$161,300
11		--------	--------	--------	--------
12	TOTAL	$499,500	$539,400	$572,000	$609,200

```
AB3: /reB7..E~
```

Fig. 6.6   The \q macro executing in STEP mode.

So far, so good. The macro correctly brings up the 1-2-3 main menu with a slash (/), correctly selects Range, and correctly selects Erase. Continue to press the space bar until 1-2-3 produces an error. (Figure 6.4 displays the error.)

OK, let's troubleshoot the problem. What was 1-2-3 supposed to do? Erase a cell. What does that involve? It involves bringing up the menu with the slash (/), selecting Range, selecting Erase, selecting the range of cells to erase, and finally pressing Enter. What went wrong? Look at the top of the screen. You can see the prompt Enter range to erase: B7..E. So, the macro correctly brought up the menu, correctly selected Range, correctly selected Erase, but an invalid range was entered. There's the problem. You can easily fix the problem by adjusting the macro to type in a valid range. To correct the error in this example, highlight cell AB3, press F2 (Edit), change the E to E10, and press Enter. (Refer to figure 6.1 for the correct macro.)

63

Stepping through a Macro That Formats Data

In Chapter 5, we created macros to format cells. In this section, we make a change to one of those macros and step through it. The result of our macro should be cells formatted to Currency with 0 Decimal Places. Retrieve the FORMAT worksheet (see fig. 6.7).

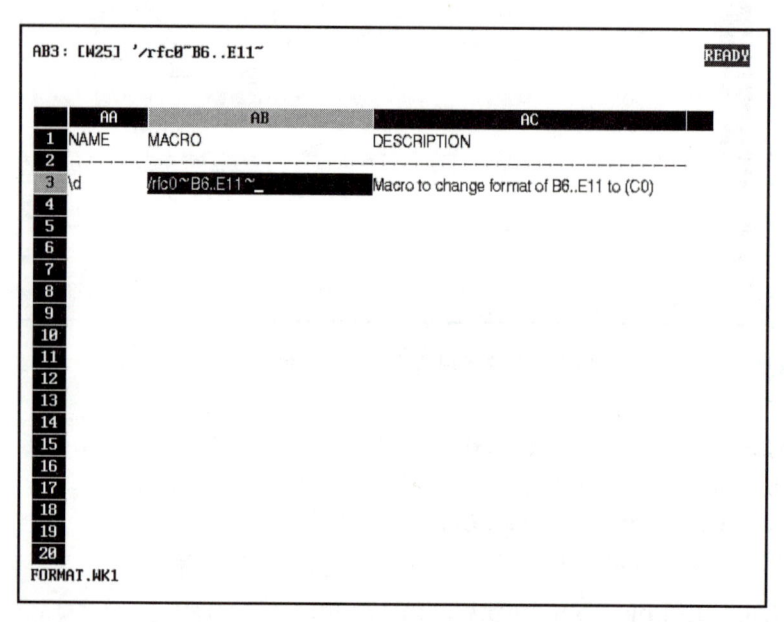

Fig. 6.7 The FORMAT worksheet with macro \d.

This macro changes the format of the range of cells B6..E11 to Currency with 0 Decimal Places. Let's make a change to the macro and then find the problem by using STEP mode. Remove the 0 (zero) following /rfc. The macro now changes the format of the range of cells B6..E11 to Currency with 2 Decimal Places. Remember that the default number of Decimal Places is 2; if you press **Enter** after selecting **C**urrency, you're selecting **2** Decimal Places. The macro should look like figure 6.8.

Testing Macros

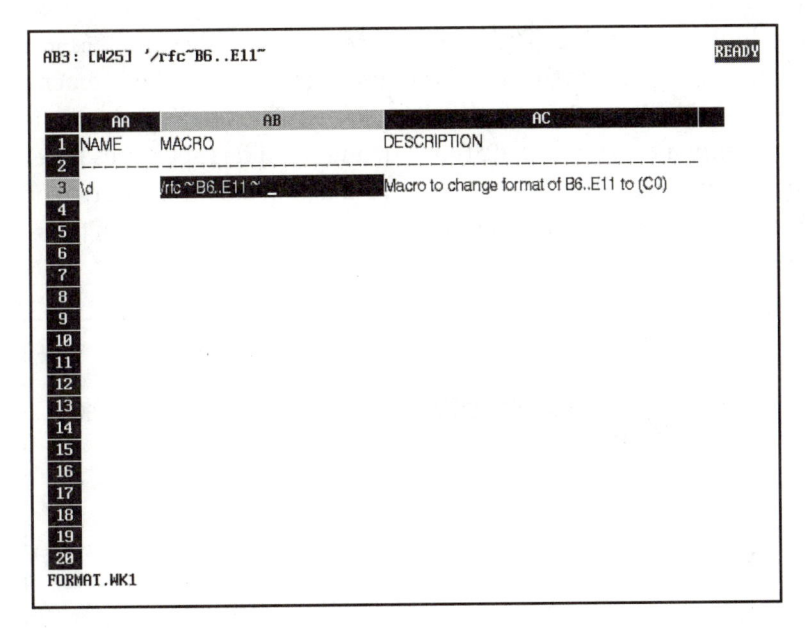

```
AB3: [W25] '/rfc~B6..E11~                                    READY

         AA              AB                          AC
   1  NAME          MACRO                    DESCRIPTION
   2  ----------------------------------------------------------
   3   \d           /rfc~B6..E11~_           Macro to change format of B6..E11 to (C0)
   4
   5
   6
   7
   8
   9
  10
  11
  12
  13
  14
  15
  16
  17
  18
  19
  20
FORMAT.WK1
```

Fig. 6.8 The modified \d macro.

Let's run the macro and see what happens. Press **Home** to move the cell pointer to cell A1. Press **Alt-D** to run the macro. The macro runs without error, and the numbers are formatted. The problem is that instead of getting numbers formatted for Currency with 0 Decimal Places, you get numbers formatted for Currency with 2 Decimal Places. That's not what we wanted or expected.

Let's step through the macro to find the problem. Press **Alt-F2** to turn on STEP mode. The STEP indicator appears at the bottom of the screen. Now run the macro by pressing **Alt-D**. The macro appears at the lower left corner of the screen. Press the **space bar** to have 1-2-3 begin stepping through the macro.

The first time you press the **space bar**, the 1-2-3 main menu appears. Press the **space bar** again and **R**ange is selected. Press the **space bar** again and **F**ormat is selected. Press the **space bar** again and **C**urrency is selected.

65

Easy 1-2-3 Macros

Now look at the screen. The prompt `Enter number of decimal places (0..15): 2` appears at the top of the screen (see fig. 6.9). Your macro appears at the lower left corner of the screen. The rectangle is on the next command to be run, the tilde (~), and the tilde (~) presses **Enter**. But you wanted 0 decimal places, not 2 decimal places. This error occurred because the macro should type **0** at this point and then press **Enter**.

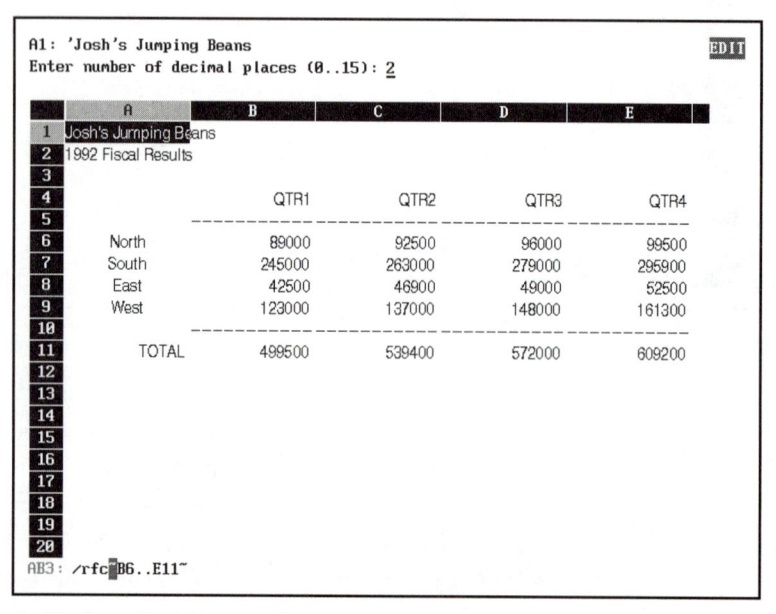

Fig. 6.9 The \d macro executing in STEP mode.

Press the **space bar** until the macro is completed. Then turn off STEP mode by pressing **Alt-F2**. To fix the macro, simply insert a `0` after `/rfc`.

OOPS! Not all macro problems create an error in 1-2-3. If the macro doesn't do what you expect, the macro has a problem and needs to be fixed.

Avoiding Common Macro Errors

A few macro errors can happen frequently. Following is a list of common errors and ways to avoid them:

Testing Macros

- *Missing characters, such as omitted tildes (~).* If you forget a tilde, which presses Enter, your macro will most likely have problems. For example, our macro to format the range B7..E10 to Currency with 0 Decimal Places in the FORMAT file is `/rfc0~B7..E10~`. If you omit the tilde after `/rfc0`, the macro doesn't press Enter to enter the number of decimal places, and 1-2-3 produces an error.

- *Spaces where they shouldn't be.* `/re~`, for example, isn't the same as `/re ~`. The space between the e and the tilde (~) creates an error when the macro is run.

- *Spelling mistakes.* A common spelling mistake is `{RIHGT}` instead of `{RIGHT}`.

Using Undo To Reverse the Effects of a Macro

1-2-3 Releases 2.2 and higher provide an Undo feature. *Undo*, as the name implies, undoes an action you have performed. For example, if you erase a cell, you can undo that erasure by pressing Alt-F4 (the Undo key). Undo can be enormously helpful if you're error prone or if you happen to be working late, and you can't handle another cup of coffee.

The Undo feature is *not* available unless you turn it on. You turn on Undo with the command /Worksheet Global Default Other Undo Enable Quit. In Releases 2.2, 2.3, and 2.4, an UNDO indicator appears at the bottom of the screen when Undo is enabled. 1-2-3 Release 3.x doesn't have an UNDO indicator; therefore, you don't know if Undo is on or not in Release 3.x until you press Alt-F4.

When Undo is enabled, you can undo the last action you performed. If the last thing you did was to enter your initials into a cell, pressing Alt-F4 removes your initials from the cell. If the last thing you did was format a cell to Currency with 2 Decimal Places, pressing Alt-F4 undoes the formatting of the cell. You can undo only the last action you performed. If you erase the contents of a cell, and then format a cell, pressing Alt-F4 removes the format of the cell because the formatting of the cell was the last action performed.

You can undo a macro just like you can undo any other worksheet command. If you press Alt-F4 after the macro finishes, you undo all worksheet changes caused by a macro. Even macros that perform multiple tasks can be undone. When you press Alt-F4, anything a macro

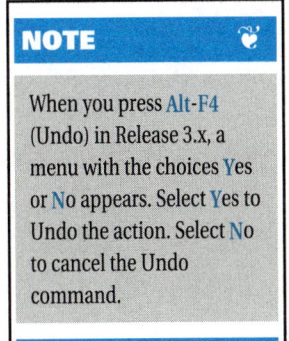

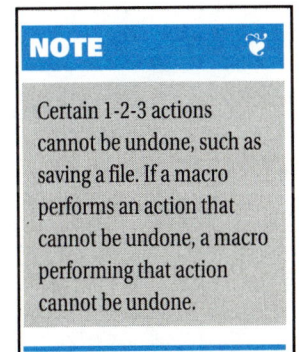

> **NOTE**
>
> When you press Alt-F4 (Undo) in Release 3.x, a menu with the choices Yes or No appears. Select Yes to Undo the action. Select No to cancel the Undo command.

> **NOTE**
>
> Certain 1-2-3 actions cannot be undone, such as saving a file. If a macro performs an action that cannot be undone, a macro performing that action cannot be undone.

does is reversed. You should always have Undo enabled when testing a macro. Macros don't always run perfectly, and they can cause a lot of problems for your worksheet. With Undo, you can revert the worksheet to its previous state (before you ran the macro). For this reason, I highly recommend you turn on Undo. Believe me, you'll be very glad you have Undo turned on if you ever need to use it!

From Here...

In this chapter, we learned how to test macros with STEP mode. We also learned about some common macro errors for you to avoid. Finally, we learned about the Undo feature and its benefits as they pertain to macros.

Next, we will explore the Learn and Record features. The 1-2-3 Release 2.x Learn feature and the 1-2-3 Release 3.x Record feature enable you to record keystrokes as you perform them.

Recording Macro Keystrokes

CHAPTER 7

Easy 1-2-3 Macros

> **NOTE**
>
> The LEARN mode is called *Record* in 1-2-3 Release 3.x. The Record feature, which works a bit differently than the LEARN mode, is explained later in this chapter. If you're using Release 3.x, skip to the section titled "Recording a Macro in Release 3.x."
>
> The LEARN mode isn't available in 1-2-3 Release 2.01 and earlier.

1-2-3 provides a *LEARN mode* that records keystrokes as you perform them. You then can place these keystrokes into your worksheet and use them as a macro. Because Learn records keystrokes as you perform them, it practically writes the macro for you. This feature can save you time and energy when creating macros; it's especially useful for lengthy keystroke macros, but you can use it to create any macro.

Defining the Learn Range

The first thing you must do to use the LEARN mode is to define the Learn range. The *Learn range* is the location where you want 1-2-3 to place the recorded keystrokes. After you define the Learn range, you activate Learn by pressing **Alt-F5**. After you press **Alt-F5**, every keystroke you perform is recorded by 1-2-3. When you turn off the LEARN mode by pressing **Alt-F5** again, Learn places the keystrokes it has recorded into the Learn range you specified.

Retrieve the LAYOUT worksheet and save the worksheet with the name LEARN. In the following example, we will define a Learn range and then activate the LEARN mode and enter some keystrokes. First, move the cell pointer to cell AB3 in the LEARN worksheet. We will make our Learn range AB3..AB4; we don't need a large Learn range because we're creating a short macro.

OOPS! Make sure that you define a Learn range that is large enough to hold all the keystrokes you're recording. If your Learn range is too small, 1-2-3 displays the error message `Learn range is full`, and you will have to redefine a larger range before you proceed. It doesn't hurt to have a Learn range that is larger than your macro requires, so you should get in the habit of defining a larger range than you think you'll need.

Each cell in the Learn range holds approximately 40 characters. Therefore, to be able to see all the recorded keystrokes, the MACROS column should be a width of 40. In the standard layout design, the MACROS column, column AB, is a width of 25. Our macros are short, so we aren't going to adjust the column width for this chapter's recorded macros.

Recording Macro Keystrokes

To define the Learn range, follow these steps:

1. Select **/W**orksheet **L**earn **R**ange.

2. Press the period (.) key to anchor the cell pointer, and press the down-arrow key once.

    Figure 7.1 shows the Learn range prompt with cells AB3..AB4 defined as the Learn range.

3. Press **Enter**.

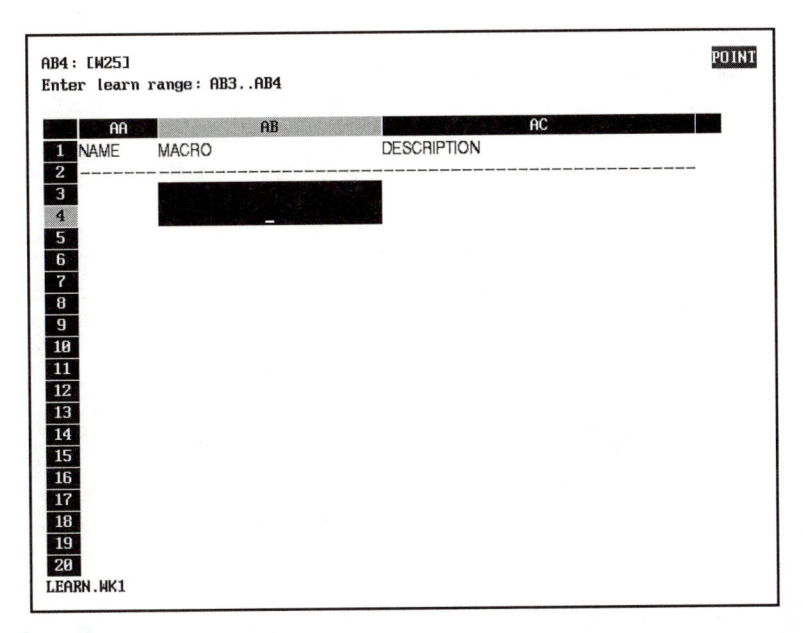

```
AB4: [W25]                                                POINT
Enter learn range: AB3..AB4

         AA          AB                    AC
  1   NAME        MACRO           DESCRIPTION
  2   ─────────────────────────────────────────
  3
  4                   _
  5
  6
  7
  8
  9
 10
 11
 12
 13
 14
 15
 16
 17
 18
 19
 20
LEARN.WK1
```

Fig. 7.1   The Learn range defined as AB3..AB4.

The Learn range now is defined as AB3..AB4. In the following sections, we're going to create a macro to type our names, move down a cell, and type our city and state. First, let's activate the LEARN mode and begin recording the keystrokes.

Activating LEARN Mode

After you specify your Learn range, you activate LEARN mode by pressing **Alt**-**F5**. When you activate LEARN mode, the LEARN indicator appears at the bottom middle of the screen. Move the cell pointer to cell A1 and press **Alt**-**F5**. Figure 7.2 shows the LEARN indicator at the bottom of the screen. Press **Alt**-**F5** again to deactivate LEARN mode.

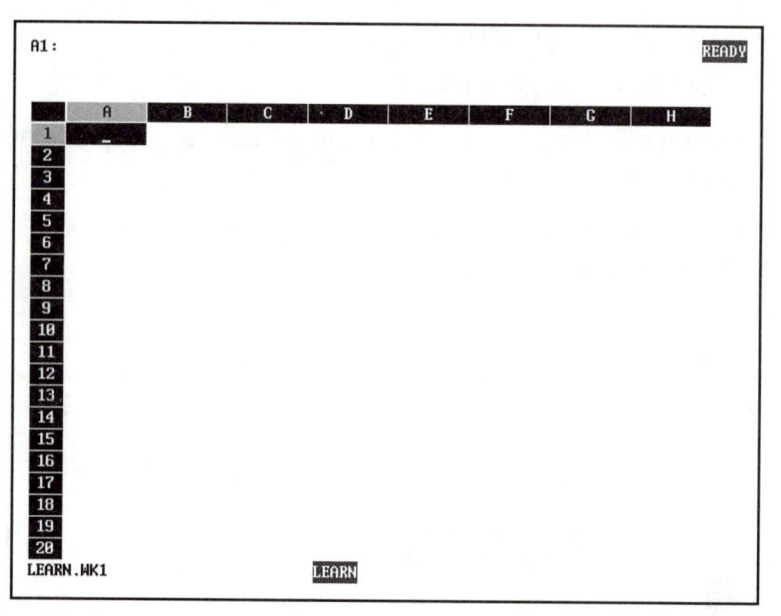

Easy 1-2-3 Macros

Fig. 7.2 The LEARN indicator at the bottom of the screen.

After you activate LEARN mode, 1-2-3 records *every* keystroke you press. If you have a dog that likes to paw your keyboard, put the dog out of the room; if the dog sets its paw on your keyboard while you're looking the other way (or if *you* rest *your* hand on the keyboard), you're going to have a lot of keystrokes recorded that you don't want or need.

Recording a Macro That Types Your Name, City, and State

In this example, we're going to type our names, press the down-arrow key, and then type our city and state.

To begin recording your keystrokes (after you have selected your Learn range), follow these steps:

1. Move the cell pointer to cell A1 if it's not already there.

2. Press **Alt-F5** to activate LEARN mode.

3. Type your name and press the down-arrow key.

   When you press the down-arrow key, your name is entered into the cell and the cell pointer moves down one cell. The cell pointer now should be in cell A2.

Recording Macro Keystrokes

4. Type the city and state in which you live and press Enter.

5. Press Alt-F5 to turn off LEARN mode.

Your keystrokes no longer are recorded after you turn off LEARN mode. When you turn off LEARN mode, the CALC indicator appears at the bottom of the screen. Press Enter to recalculate the worksheet and place the recorded keystrokes in the Learn range. I'm not sure why 1-2-3 doesn't just dump the keystrokes into the Learn range automatically, but it doesn't. (Pressing Enter, however, ensures that the keystrokes are placed in the Learn range.)

Move the cell pointer to cell AA1 so we can see the keystrokes entered in the Learn range. Remember that we defined our Learn range as AB3..AB4 and—ta da!—the recorded keystrokes appear in cell AB3. As it turns out, we didn't need AB4 because this was a short macro. Let me reiterate that having too large a range doesn't cause any problems, and you should always create a larger Learn range than the macro requires.

Figure 7.3 shows the recorded keystrokes entered in cell AB3. You can see your name, the {D} for the down arrow (which entered your name and moved the cell pointer down), and finally your city and state. The tilde presses Enter to enter the city and state.

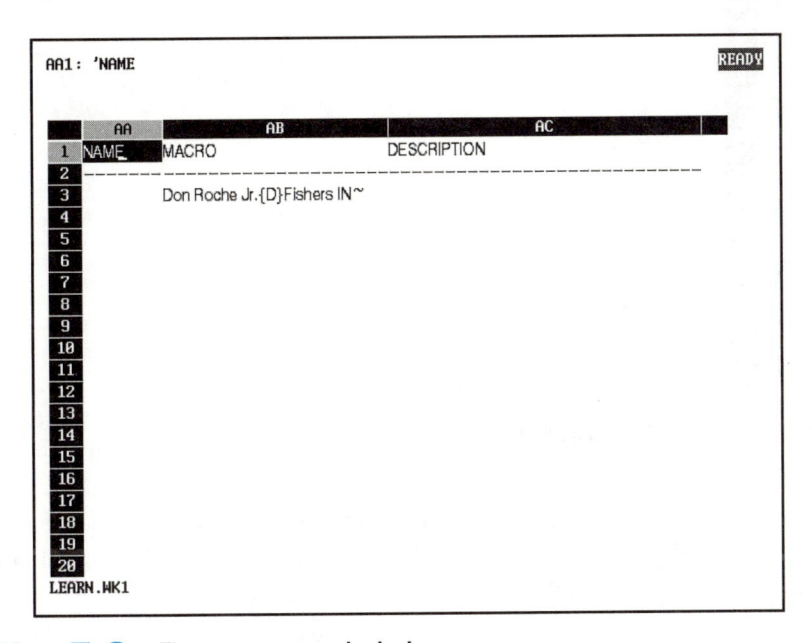

Fig. 7.3 The macro appears in the Learn range.

Easy 1-2-3 Macros

As you remember from Chapter 2, all macros must have a name or they can't be run.

To name and document the macro you just created, follow these steps:

1. To name the macro, move the cell pointer to cell AA3.

2. Type '\n and press Enter.

   Because the macro enters your name, city, and state, we will name the macro \n.

3. Select /Range Name Labels Right and press Enter.

4. To document the macro, move the cell pointer to cell AC3.

5. Type Macro to enter name, city, and state and press Enter.

Figure 7.4 shows the completed macro.

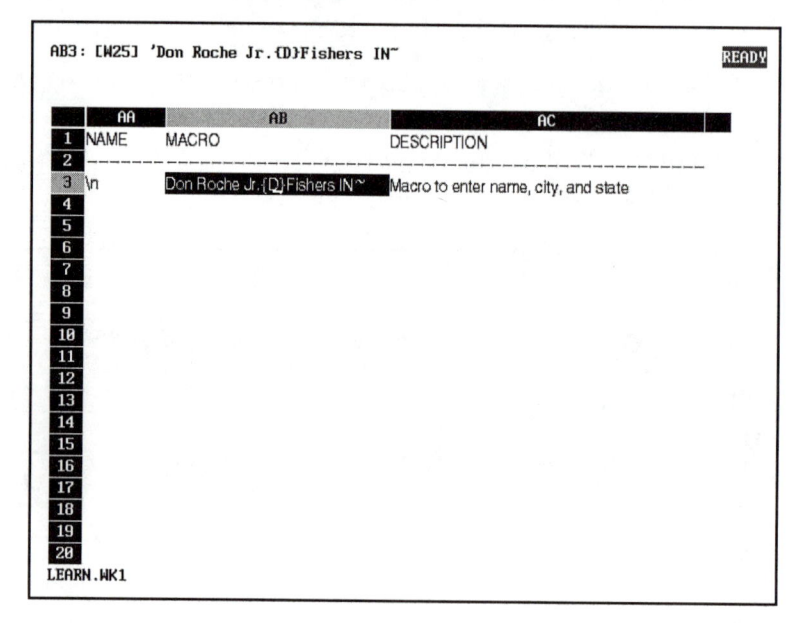

Fig. 7.4   The completed \n macro.

Now we'll move to a blank area of the worksheet and run the macro. Move the cell pointer to cell A40, which is a blank area of the worksheet, and press Alt-N to run the macro. Figure 7.5 shows the results.

Recording Macro Keystrokes

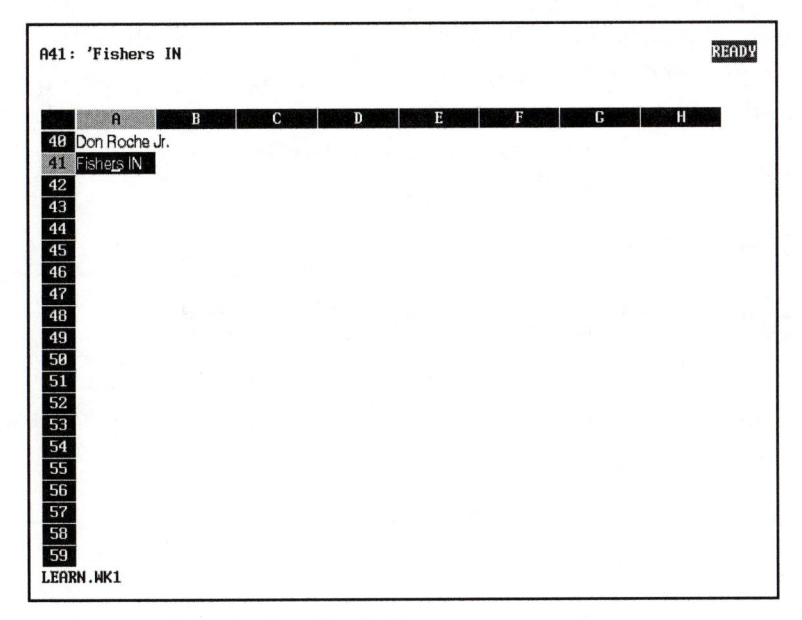

```
A41: 'Fishers IN                                    READY

      A         B      C      D      E      F      G      H
 40 Don Roche Jr.
 41 Fishers IN
 42
 43
 44
 45
 46
 47
 48
 49
 50
 51
 52
 53
 54
 55
 56
 57
 58
 59
LEARN.WK1
```

Fig. 7.5   The result of running the \n macro.

OOPS! Because every keystroke you press is recorded by LEARN mode, even the ones you press accidentally or press to delete a mistake are recorded. If you begin to type your name and see that you accidentally type an *e* rather than an *a*, for example, you have to press Backspace to delete the *e* and you have to type an *a*. When you finish recording the macro and the recorded keystrokes are placed in the Learn range, that sequence will appear as e{BS}a; the {BS} represents the Backspace key. This isn't a problem because you get the desired result when the macro is run because Learn recorded your fixing the mistake. When you're more comfortable with macros, you can edit the mistakes and record "fixes" to clean up the macros.

OOPS! In 1-2-3 Release 2.2, keystrokes in the Allways add-in are not recorded by LEARN mode. If you attach the Allways add-in in Release 2.2, be aware that menu commands from the Allways menu aren't recorded by LEARN mode.

75

Easy 1-2-3 Macros

You should always press the first letter of the command rather than move the cell pointer to the command and press Enter when you record a macro. This action makes the macro easier to understand and debug. This action also requires fewer keystrokes.

Recording a Macro That Saves a Worksheet

In the next example, we'll record a macro with the LEARN mode that will save the current file. First, retrieve the LAYOUT worksheet and save it with the name SAVEMAC.

To record the macro with the LEARN mode, follow these steps:

1. Move the cell pointer to cell AB3.

2. Select /Worksheet Learn Range.

3. Highlight the Learn range AB3..AB4 and press Enter.

   A two-cell Learn range will be large enough because this macro is short.

4. Press Alt-F5 to activate LEARN mode.

5. Select /File Save, press Enter, and select Replace.

   This action saves the current version of the worksheet and replaces the old version.

6. Press Alt-F5 to turn off LEARN mode. Press Enter to recalculate the worksheet and place the recorded keystrokes into the Learn range.

Figure 7.6 shows the recorded keystrokes in cell AB3.

Recording Macro Keystrokes

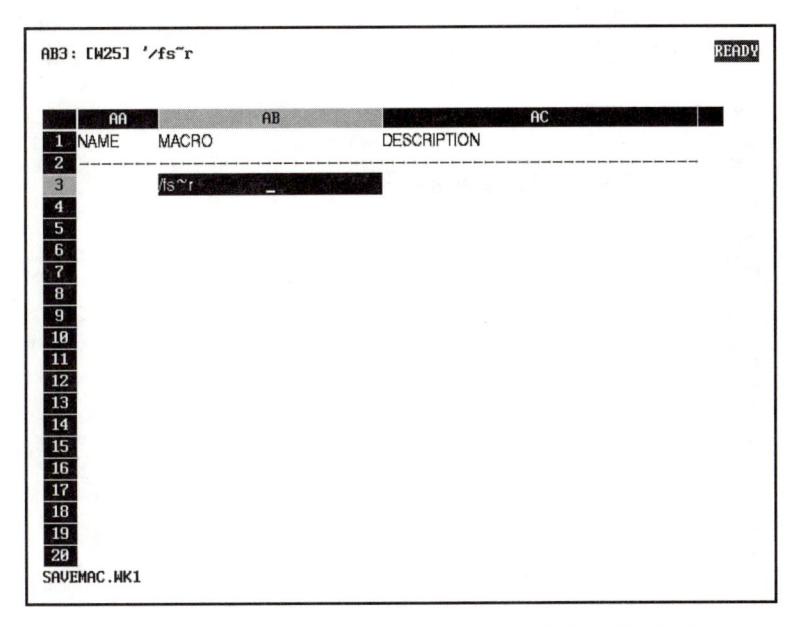

```
AB3: [W25]  '/fs~r                                    READY

         AA            AB                   AC
    1  NAME         MACRO              DESCRIPTION
    2  ─────────────────────────────────────────────────
    3               /fs~r
    4
    5
    6
    7
    8
    9
   10
   11
   12
   13
   14
   15
   16
   17
   18
   19
   20
   SAVEMAC.WK1
```

Fig. 7.6 The keystrokes to save a file recorded and placed in the Learn range.

Now we must name and document the macro. Follow these steps:

1. To name the macro, move the cell pointer to cell AA3.

2. Type **'\s** and press **Enter**.

   Because the macro saves a file, we will name the macro \s.

3. Select **/R**ange **N**ame **L**abels **R**ight and press **Enter**.

4. To document the macro, first move the cell pointer to cell AC3.

5. Type **Macro to save the current file** and press **Enter**.

Figure 7.7 shows the completed macro.

Easy 1-2-3 Macros

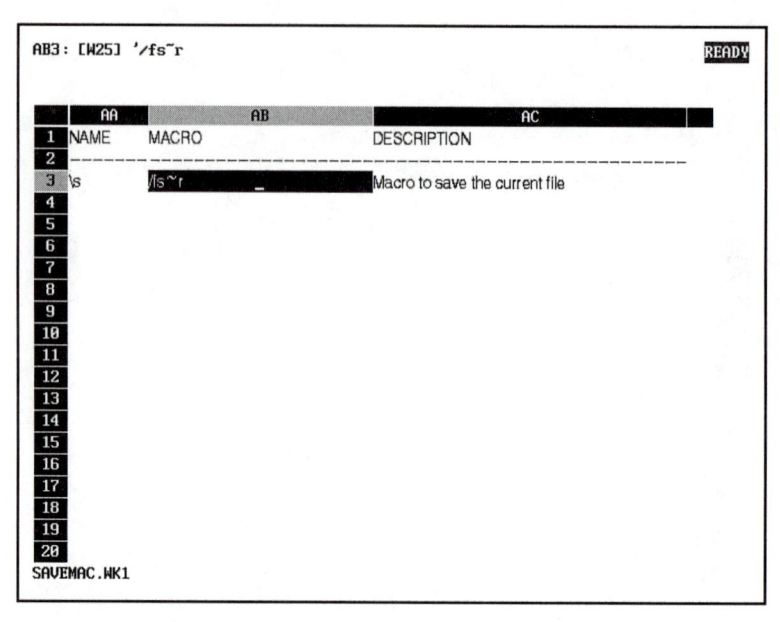

Fig. 7.7 The completed \s macro.

Now when you need to save this file, all you have to do is press **Alt-S**. Nice and simple!

Recording a Macro That Changes the File Directory

You frequently need to change the file directory you're retrieving files from and saving files to. If you have a computer with a drive C, for example, you normally retrieve and save files to drive C. When a co-worker gives you a floppy disk with a file to work on, you need to retrieve the file from drive A and save the file back to drive A. A macro that changes the directory so that 1-2-3 retrieves and saves files from and to drive A can be very helpful. We're going to use LEARN mode to write a macro to change the directory.

First, retrieve the LAYOUT worksheet and save the worksheet with the name DIRECT. We now will record a macro with the LEARN mode that will change the current file directory.

Recording Macro Keystrokes

To record the macro, follow these steps:

1. Move the cell pointer to cell AB3.

2. Select /Worksheet Learn Range.

3. Highlight the Learn range AB3..AB4 and press Enter.

   A two-cell Learn range will be large enough because this is a short macro.

4. Press Alt-F5 to activate LEARN mode.

5. Select /File Directory, type a:, and press Enter.

   This action changes the file directory to drive A.

6. Press Alt-F5 to turn off LEARN mode. Press Enter to recalculate the worksheet and place the recorded keystrokes into the Learn range.

Figure 7.8 shows the recorded keystrokes in cell AB3.

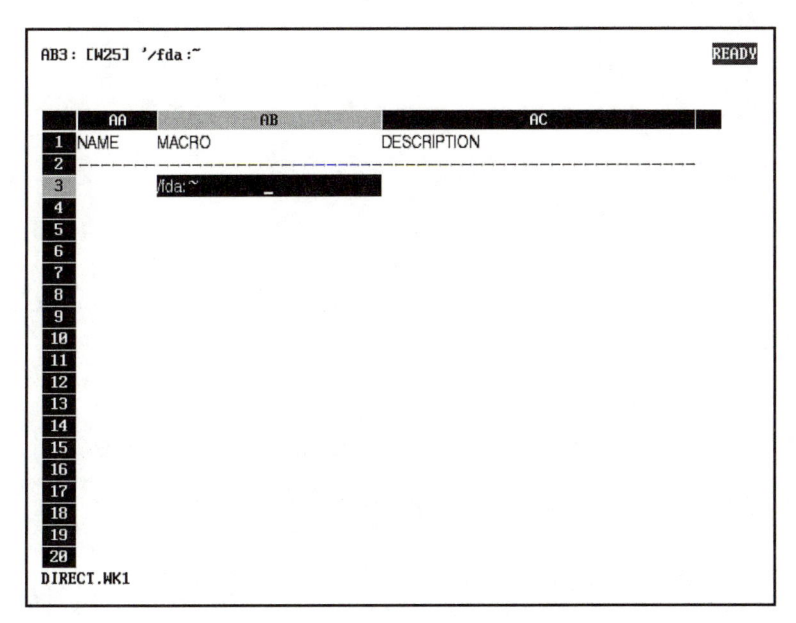

Fig. 7.8 The macro to change the file directory to drive A.

Now we must name and document the macro. Follow these steps:

1. To name the macro, move the cell pointer to cell AA3.

2. Type '\a and press Enter.

   Because this macro changes the file directory to A, we will name the macro \a.

Easy 1-2-3 Macros

3. Select **/R**ange **N**ame **L**abels **R**ight and press **Enter**.

4. To document the macro, move the cell pointer to cell AC3.

5. Type **Macro to change the file directory to A:** and press **Enter**.

Figure 7.9 shows the completed macro.

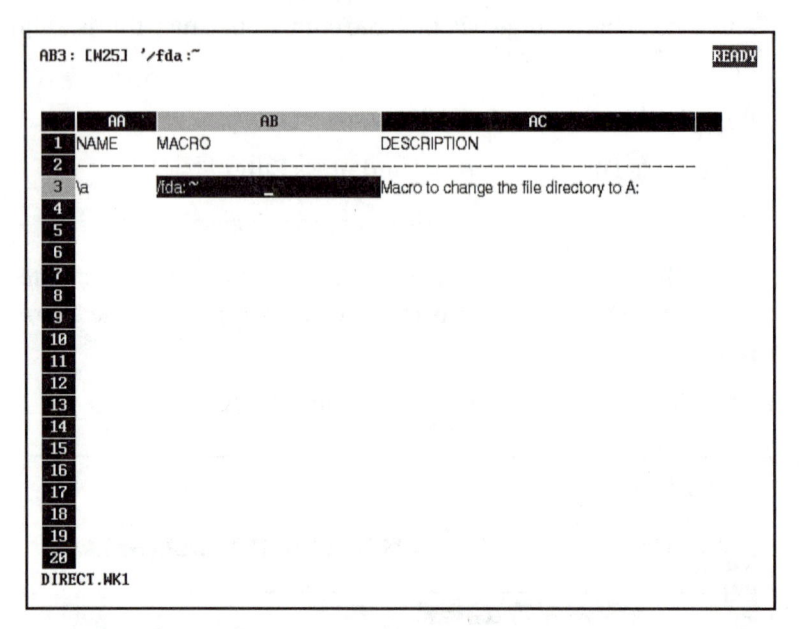

Fig. 7.9 The completed \a macro.

As I hope you have learned so far in this chapter, the LEARN mode of 1-2-3 can be enormously helpful when creating macros.

Recording a Macro in 1-2-3 Release 3.x

1-2-3 Release 3.x also offers a feature that records keystrokes, but it works quite a bit differently than the LEARN mode in Release 2.x. The Release 3.x feature is called *Record*. You don't have to activate Record because it's always on. *All* your keystrokes in Release 3.x are recorded, regardless of whether you use them for anything. The keystrokes are recorded in the *record buffer*, which is where 1-2-3 keeps track of the keystrokes. **Alt-F2** is the key combination you use to work with Record.

1-2-3 Release 2.x worksheets can be retrieved into Release 3.x, so we can simply retrieve the LAYOUT worksheet. Save the worksheet with

Recording Macro Keystrokes

the name RECORD. We will create a macro to enter our names by using the Release 3.x Record feature.

To record the macro, follow these steps:

1. Press **Alt-F2**.

   The Record menu appears, as shown in figure 7.10.

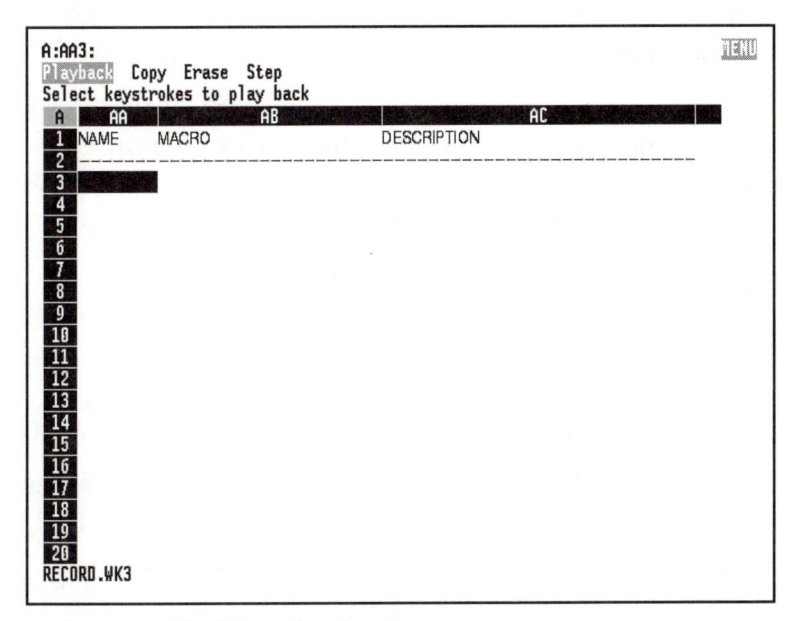

Fig. 7.10   The Release 3.x Record menu.

2. Select **E**rase.

   Erase clears out anything that Record has recorded up to that point. You always should select **E**rase before you begin to record the keystrokes for your macro. You don't want any keystrokes other than the ones you enter for the macro that will be stored in the record buffer.

OOPS! It's important to select **E**rase before you begin to record the keystrokes for your macro. If you don't select **E**rase, you will have many keystrokes in the record buffer that aren't related to your macro. Remember that Record is on all the time; every keystroke you've made since you started 1-2-3 has been recorded. If you don't select **E**rase to clear the record buffer, you will have a hard time copying the correct macro keystrokes to the worksheet.

81

Easy 1-2-3 Macros

3. Perform the keystrokes for the macro.

   We will record the keystrokes to type our names. Move the cell pointer to cell A1. Type your name and press **Enter**. Now the keystrokes for our macro are in the record buffer. Remember that you don't turn on Record—it's on all the time.

4. Move the cell pointer back to cell AB3, which is where we will put the keystrokes we have just recorded. Press **F5** (GoTo) to move to cell AA1, and then press the arrow keys to move to cell AB3.

   It's important that you move the cell pointer to cell AB3 by using the method described here. This action ensures that you can see your macro standard layout design when you copy your keystrokes to the worksheet. We will place the recorded keystrokes for our macro in cell AB3.

5. Press **Alt-F2** to bring up the Record menu and select **C**opy.

   The Copy choice enables you to copy keystrokes that are in the record buffer to the worksheet. Figure 7.11 shows the keystrokes that are in the record buffer. As you can see, the keystrokes appear at the top of the screen, and our worksheet is shortened to accommodate the record buffer.

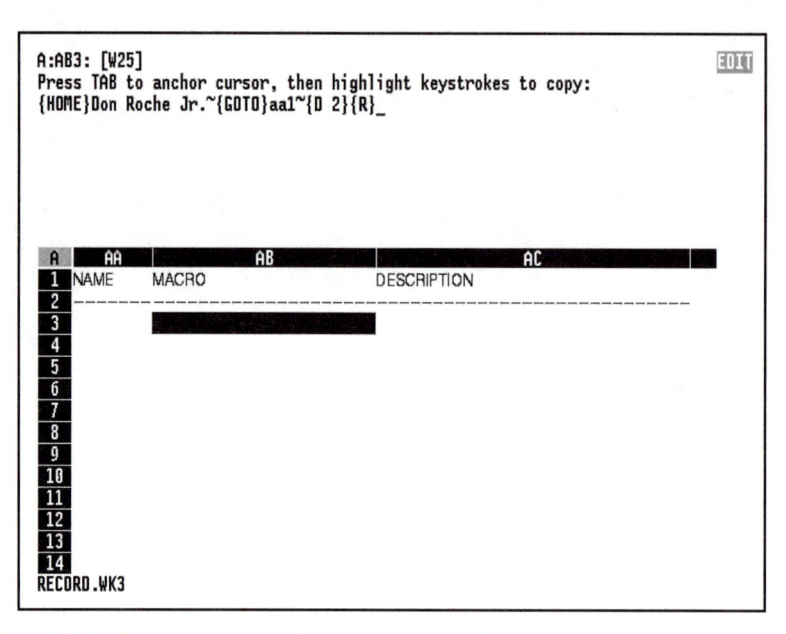

> **NOTE**
>
> The record buffer can hold up to 512 keystrokes.

Fig. 7.11 The record buffer after selecting **C**opy.

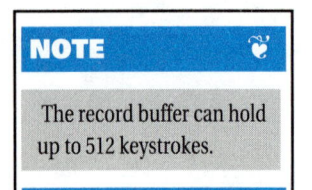

Recording Macro Keystrokes

As you can see, the record buffer contains more keystrokes than we want for our macro. We only want the keystrokes that type our names. But all the keystrokes we have made since clearing the record buffer with the Erase command are in the buffer. The Copy command, however, enables you to highlight only the keystrokes you need and copy only those keystrokes to the worksheet for the macro.

The prompt at the top of the screen tells you to `Press TAB to anchor cursor, then highlight keystrokes to copy:`.

You need to move the cursor, which is currently at the end of the recorded keystrokes, to the correct position so that you highlight only your name followed by the tilde (~). Press the left-arrow key until the cursor is under the tilde. Then press Tab. This action anchors the cursor so when you press an arrow key, you will be highlighting rather than moving the cursor. Press the left-arrow key until the highlight expands across your name. If you press Tab at the wrong location, press Esc to unanchor the cursor and start over. Figure 7.12 shows my name highlighted.

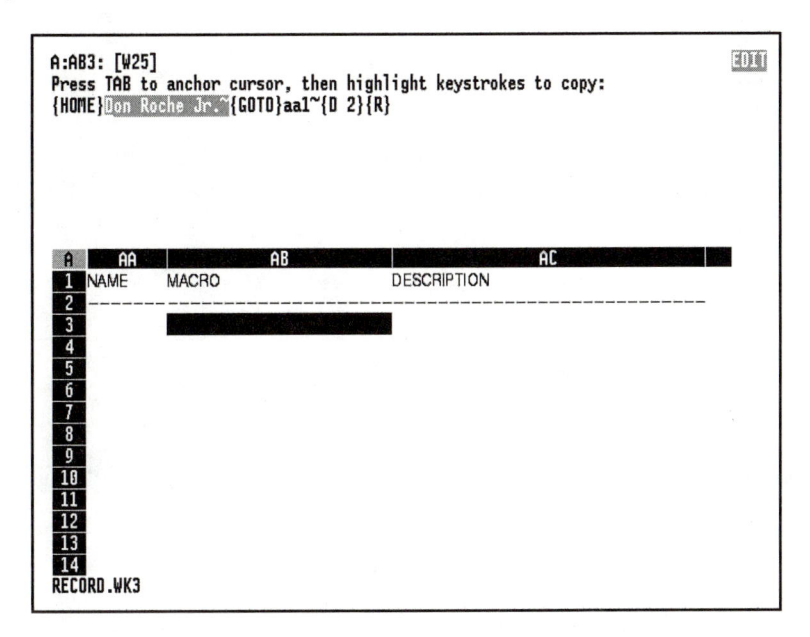

Fig. 7.12 The highlighted keystrokes to copy for the macro.

Easy 1-2-3 Macros

OOPS! You must be careful to highlight *only* the keystrokes that make up your macro after you select Copy from the record buffer. All the highlighted keystrokes are copied to the worksheet. If, after you copy the keystrokes, you end up with keystrokes that aren't supposed to be in the macro, use F2 (Edit) to remove the unwanted keystrokes.

After you highlight the keystrokes you want to copy to the worksheet, press Enter. The highlighted keystrokes are entered into cell AB3. Figure 7.13 shows the keystrokes for our macro entered in cell AB3.

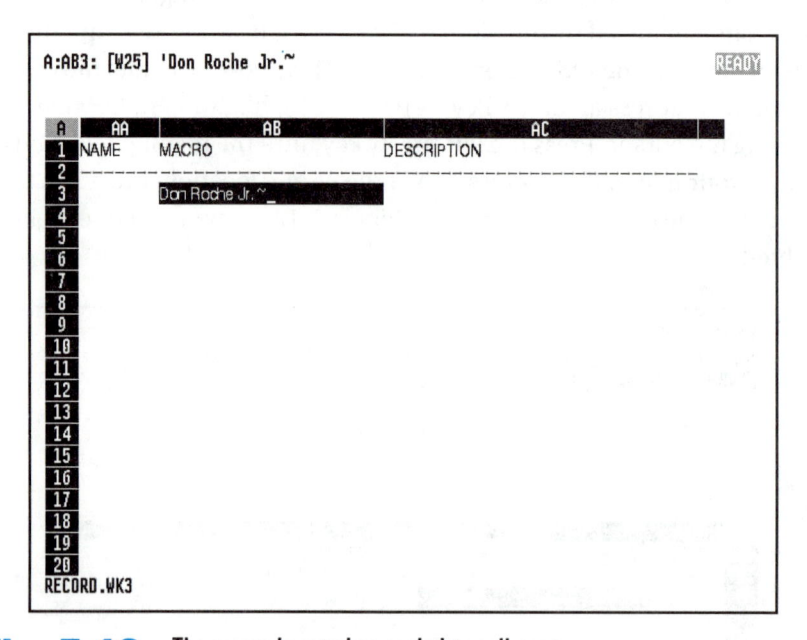

Fig. 7.13 The macro keystrokes copied to cell AB3.

Now, just like we had to do when we recorded our macro using LEARN mode, we must name and document the macro. Follow these steps:

1. To name the macro, move the cell pointer to cell AA3.
2. Type '\n and press Enter.

   Because this macro enters your name, we will name it \n.

3. Select /Range Name Labels Right and press Enter.
4. To document the macro, move the cell pointer to cell AC3.
5. Type Macro to enter my name and press Enter.

84

Figure 7.14 shows the completed macro.

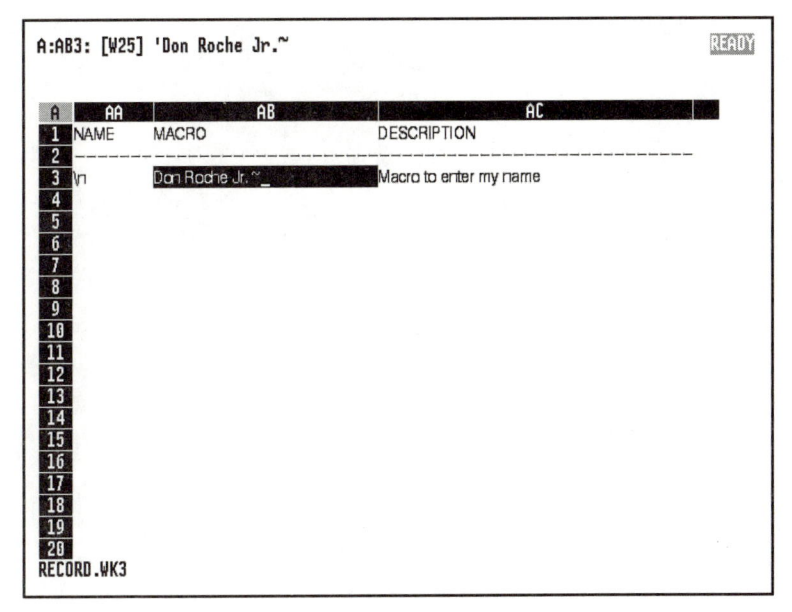

Fig. 7.14 The completed \n macro in Release 3.x.

From Here...

In this chapter, you learned how to record a macro by using the Release 2.x LEARN mode and the Release 3.x Record feature. Both of these 1-2-3 capabilities facilitate macro writing because the keystrokes for the macro are written by 1-2-3.

Next, we'll learn how to use the Macro Library Manager add-in. The Macro Library Manager add-in enables you to use your macros with any worksheet, not just the worksheet in which you created the macro.

Using the Macro Library Manager with Release 2.x

CHAPTER 8

Easy 1-2-3 Macros

The *Macro Library Manager* is a 1-2-3 Release 2.x add-in that enables you to use your macros with any 1-2-3 worksheet. You can have only one worksheet in memory at a time with Release 2.x. Therefore, when you create a macro in a worksheet, only that worksheet can run the macro. You can't run the macro in any other worksheet. The Macro Library Manager, however, enables you to share any macro with any worksheet. The immediate benefit of being able to share your macros is that you only have to write them once!

An *add-in*, as the name implies, is something that isn't part of the core 1-2-3 program, but something you "add-in" to 1-2-3. Lotus gives you certain add-ins with 1-2-3, and the Macro Library Manager is one of them. Therefore, you don't have to spend extra money for the add-in! The Macro Library Manager isn't automatically available when you load 1-2-3. You have to select /Add-In and add the Macro Library Manager into memory so that 1-2-3 can use it. The next section discusses how to accomplish this task.

The Macro Library Manager creates a special Macro Library File. You can have multiple library files that you can use when the Macro Library Manager is added to 1-2-3. After adding the Macro Library Manager, you load Macro Library files, one or several, into the Macro Library Manager. All the macros in the Macro Library file will then be available to any worksheet.

> **NOTE**
>
> Release 3.x doesn't have a Macro Library Manager add-in because there is no need for it. Because Release 3.x enables you to have multiple worksheets in memory at the same time, simply place your macros in a macro worksheet and place that worksheet in memory. Any worksheet can then use the macros.

OOPS! The Macro Library Manager add-in will take up memory you may need for worksheet data. You may not want to use the add-in if you're working with a large worksheet.

Adding the Macro Library Manager

Lotus refers to adding any add-in as attaching the add-in. It doesn't matter where the cell pointer is when you attach an add-in since you're simply loading something into memory.

Using the Macro Library Manager with Release 2.x

To attach the Macro Library Manager add-in, follow these steps:

1. Select **/A**dd-In **A**ttach.

    The list of available add-ins appears below the prompt `Enter add-in to attach:` (see fig. 8.1). The MACROMGR.ADN add-in is included in this list. All add-ins have an ADN extension.

    The 1-2-3 directory on your machine (which is `C:\123R23` for me and will be for you unless you changed it during the installation of 1-2-3 onto your machine) appears after the prompt.

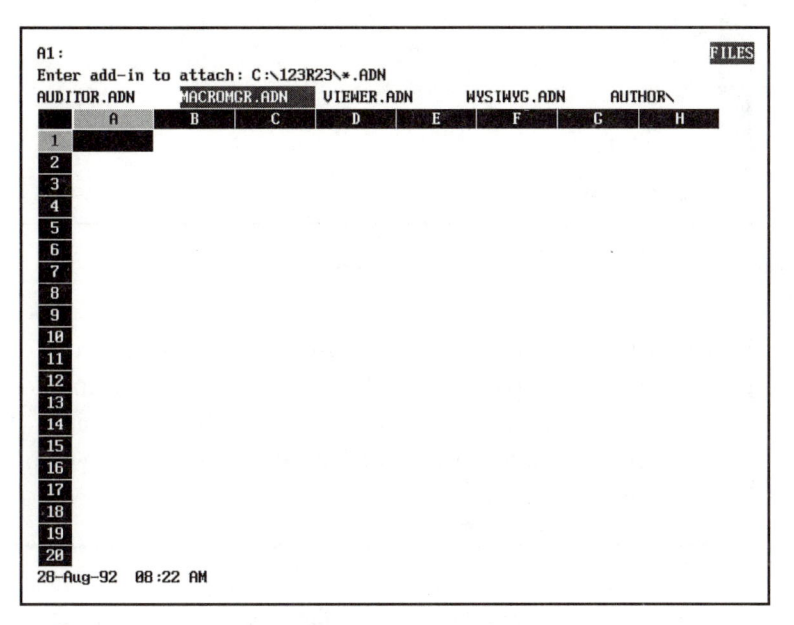

Fig. 8.1 The list of available add-ins after selecting **/A**dd-In **A**ttach.

2. Highlight `MACROMGR.ADN` and press **Enter**. The list of key combinations available for you to invoke the Macro Library Manager menu after it's attached appears (see fig. 8.2). (You press **7** to assign **A**lt-**F7**, press **8** to assign **A**lt-**F8**, press **9** to assign **A**lt-**F9**, and press **1** to assign **A**lt-**F10**.)

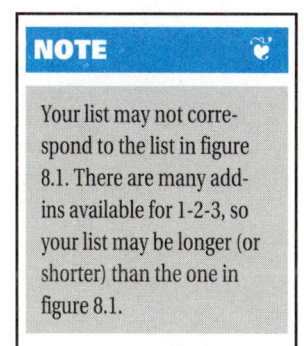

> **NOTE**
>
> Your list may not correspond to the list in figure 8.1. There are many add-ins available for 1-2-3, so your list may be longer (or shorter) than the one in figure 8.1.

Easy 1-2-3 Macros

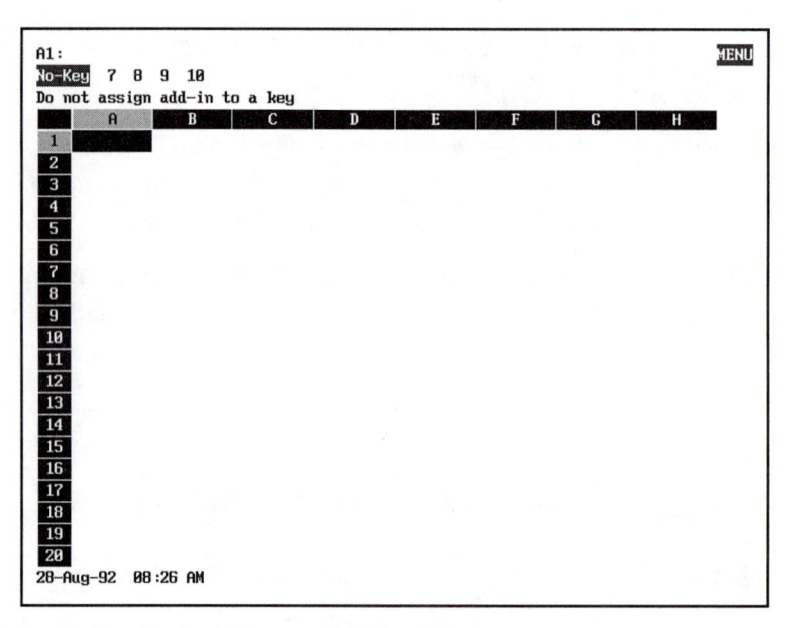

Fig. 8.2 The list of keys available for invoking the add-in.

It's easier to assign a key combination—choices 7 through 10—that invokes the Macro Library Manager menu than it is to select No-Key. You have multiple key-combination choices because you can have multiple add-ins attached at the same time. The following list explains each choice:

Key	Function
No-Key	Enables you to invoke the Macro Library Manager each time through the menu (not a key combination). If you select No-Key, you must invoke the Macro Library Manager menu by selecting /Add-In Invoke.
7	Enables you to invoke the Macro Library Manager menu by pressing Alt-F7.
8	Enables you to invoke the Macro Library Manager menu by pressing Alt-F8.
9	Enables you to invoke the Macro Library Manager menu by pressing Alt-F9.
10	Enables you to invoke the Macro Library Manager menu by pressing Alt-F10.

3. Press 7.

The preceding step enables you to invoke the Macro Library Manager menu by pressing Alt-F7.

Using the Macro Library Manager with Release 2.x

4. Select Quit.

   The Macro Library Manager add-in is attached and available for use. Now all we have to do is create a macro library!

Creating a Macro Library

You create a macro library simply by creating a group of macros in a worksheet and then saving those macros as a library file. So, first we need to create a few macros. Retrieve the LAYOUT worksheet and save the worksheet with the name LIBRARY. We will use a couple of the macros we created earlier in the book: a macro that erases data and a macro that formats a cell to Currency with 2 Decimal Places. Figure 8.3 shows the macros to create for the library. There are two macros in the file. Create these macros in the LIBRARY worksheet. Make sure that you remember to name the macros with the /Range Name Labels Right command. (Refer to Chapter 3 to review the macro to erase data; refer to Chapter 5 to review the macro to format cells to Currency with 2 Decimal Places.)

> **NOTE**
>
> If there are other add-ins attached to 1-2-3 and they have been assigned key combinations, your key-combination list may not be the same as that in figure 8.2. If a key combination is in use, 1-2-3 doesn't display that key combination in the list. If you have the Wysiwyg add-in (Releases 2.3 and 2.4) attached to Alt-F7, for example, the number 7 doesn't appear in the key-combination list when you attach the Macro Library Manager.

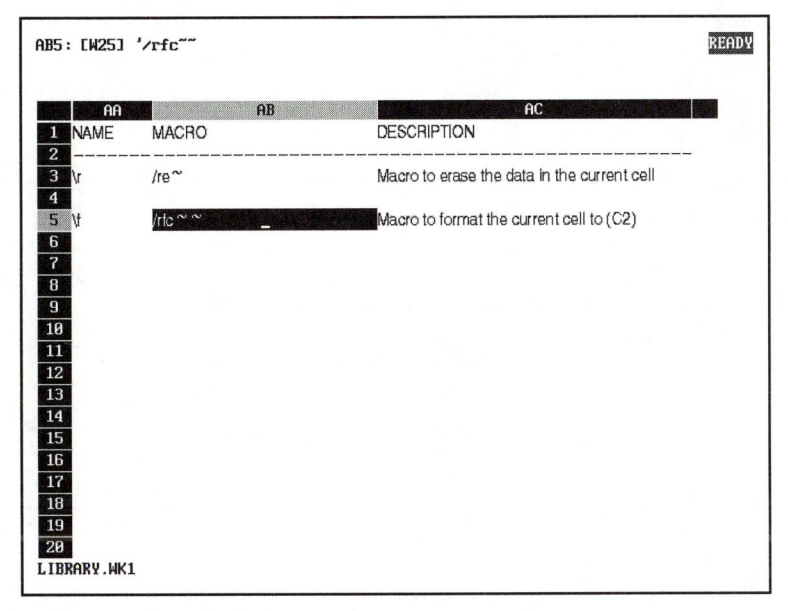

Fig. 8.3 The macros to place in a Macro Library file.

Easy 1-2-3 Macros

Now that we have the macros, we can save them as a library file. Follow these steps:

1. Move the cell pointer to cell AA3, the cell location of the first macro name.

2. You must invoke the Macro Library Manager menu in order to save the macros as a library file. Because you selected 7 when you attached the add-in, you can invoke the menu by pressing Alt-F7.

   Figure 8.4 shows the Macro Library Manager menu.

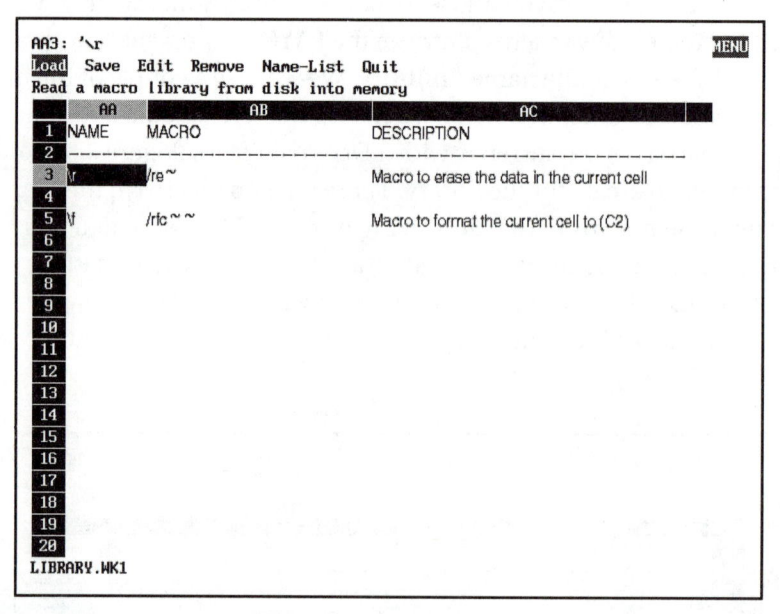

Fig. 8.4   The Macro Library Manager menu.

3. Select Save from the Macro Library Manager menu.

4. Next, you must provide a name for the library. Let's name this library GENERAL because the two macros perform general worksheet tasks. Type general and press Enter.

5. You now must provide the macro library range, which is simply the location of our macros. Highlight cells AA3..AC5 and press Enter.

   Figure 8.5 shows the highlighted range for our Macro Library file.

Using the Macro Library Manager with Release 2.x

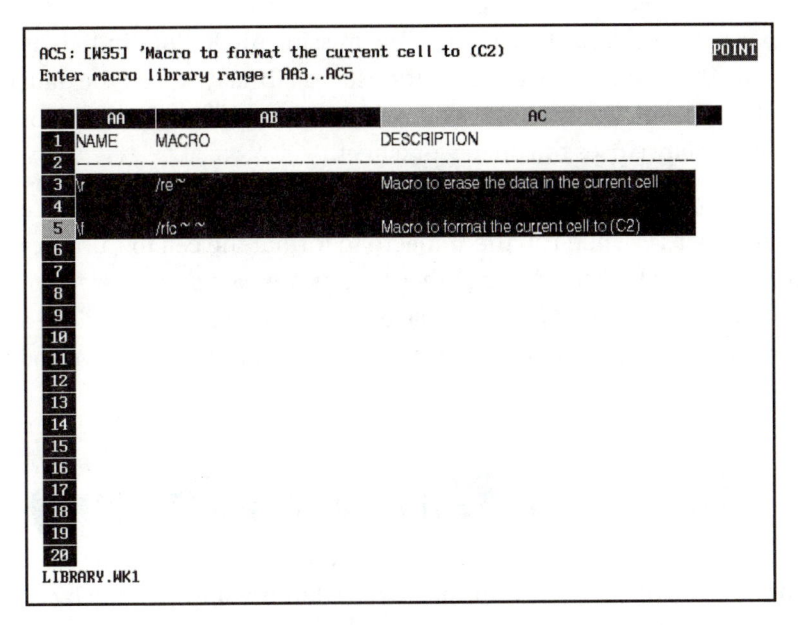

Fig. 8.5 The macros highlighted for the Macro Library file.

You can password-protect your library files. This process prevents anyone from editing your files unless they know the password.

6. After you highlight the range containing the macros and you press Enter, you are offered Yes and No choices at the `Use password to lock library:` prompt. Select No.

The macros in the selected range disappear from the screen. As you can see, the macros are not copied but are removed from the file and placed into the Macro Library file named GENERAL. Now you have two macros in a Macro Library file named GENERAL. At this point, you can use these two macros with any worksheet you retrieve or any new worksheet. If you select Yes to password-protect the file, you are prompted for a password. Type in a password (it can be up to 15 characters), and when you press Enter, the macros in the selected range are removed from the file and are placed in the Macro Library file.

Let's see the macros work. Bring up a brand new worksheet by selecting the /Worksheet Erase Yes Yes command. Remember, the Macro Library file is still in memory. The Library file is in memory until we remove it. The /WEYY command only brings up a new worksheet. Now we have a brand new, blank worksheet. Type your initials in cell A1. Then run the

93

Easy 1-2-3 Macros

\r macro—the Erase Data macro—by pressing **Alt-R**. Your initials are erased. The \r macro, which is in the Macro Library, erased the data in the current cell. (Remember, when you bring up a worksheet, 1-2-3 automatically closes the open worksheet.)

Let's try the Format macro. Move the cell pointer to cell A5 and enter the number **10**. Then run the \f macro to format the cell to Currency with 2 Decimal Places. The number 10 now appears as `$10.00`, formatted to Currency with 2 Decimal Places. Any worksheet you retrieve and any new worksheet can use the macros. This capability can save you a lot of time!

Editing a Macro Library

Your macros don't become untouchable after they're in a Macro Library file. You can edit your macros in a Library file any time by choosing **E**dit from the Macro Library Manager menu. Let's edit our Format macro so that it formats a cell for Currency with 0 Decimal Places rather than Currency with 2 Decimal Places.

The first thing you always do before editing a Macro Library file is save your current worksheet and bring up a blank worksheet with the **/W**orksheet **E**rase **Y**es **Y**es command. Now that you've done that, let's edit our macro.

To edit the macro, follow these steps:

1. Press **Alt-F7** to bring up the Macro Library Manager menu and select **E**dit.

   A list of the libraries that are in memory appears under the prompt `Enter name of macro library to edit:` (see fig. 8.6). The only library file we have created and saved, `GENERAL` (which appears as `GENERAL.MLB`) appears as the only file to edit.

Using the Macro Library Manager with Release 2.x

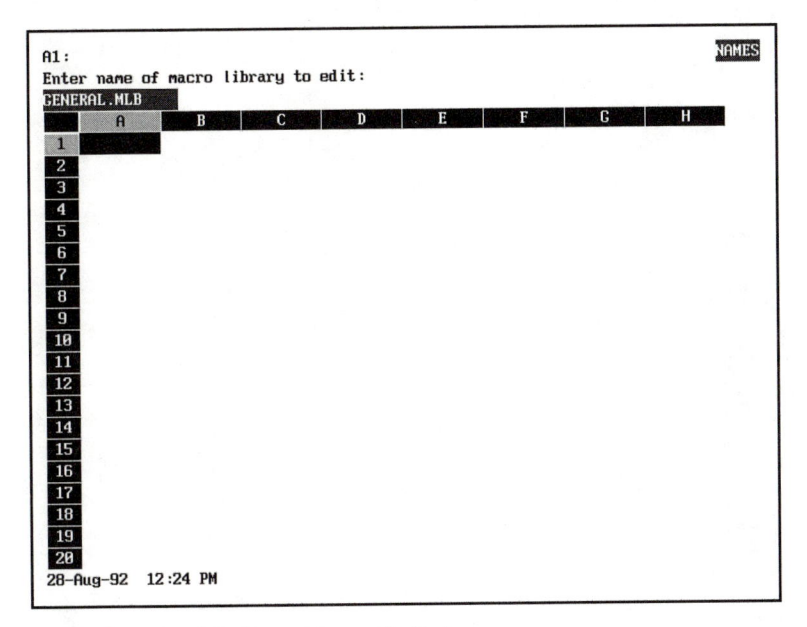

Fig. 8.6 The Edit Macro Library file listing.

2. Highlight **GENERAL** and press **Enter**. Then select **I**gnore.

   Actually, it doesn't matter whether you select **I**gnore or **O**verwrite because we cleared the worksheet with the **/W**orksheet **E**rase command. A brand new worksheet doesn't have any range names to create any problems—that is why we always clear the worksheet before editing a library file.

3. Because this is a blank worksheet, you don't have to worry about overwriting any data, so you can simply press **Enter** at the `Enter range for macro library:` prompt.

   This step is another benefit of erasing the worksheet before editing a library file. Figure 8.7 shows the macros copied from the Macro Library Manager to your worksheet for editing.

95

Easy 1-2-3 Macros

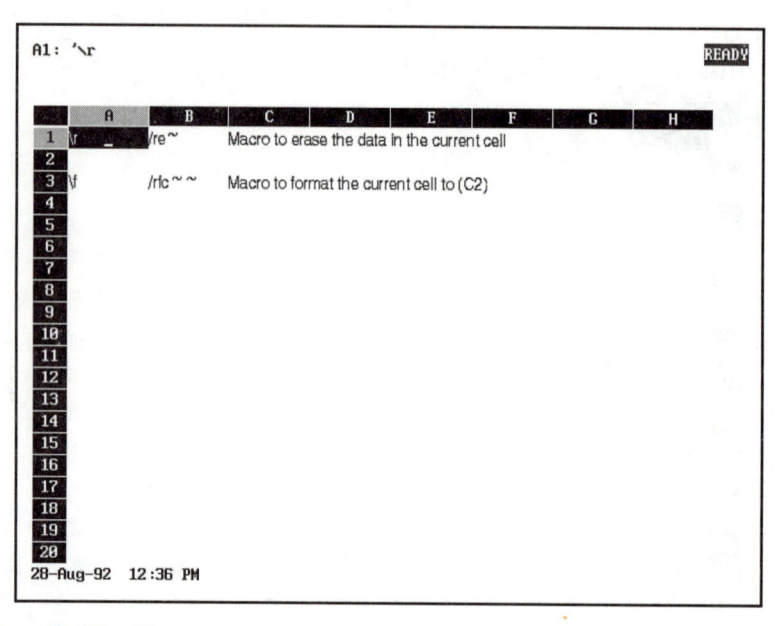

Fig. 8.7   The macros copied into the worksheet for editing.

Now, we simply edit the macro. Move the cell pointer to cell B3, which is the cell with the Format macro, and edit the macro so that it reads `'/rfc0~~`. The macro now will format a cell for Currency with 0 Decimal Places rather than Currency with 2 Decimal Places.

After editing the macro, you resave it to the GENERAL.MLB macro library file.

To save the modified macro to the Macro Library, follow these steps:

1. Move the cell pointer to cell A1, which is the cell location of the first macro name.

2. Press **Alt**-**F7** to invoke the Macro Library Manager menu and select **S**ave. Any library files you save appear under the prompt `Enter name of Macro Library to save`.

3. Since we are saving the changed macro to the GENERAL.MLB file, highlight the macro library name **GENERAL** and press **Enter**.

    In this example, we're not creating a new library file—we're replacing an old one.

4. When the next prompt appears with the choices **N**o or **Y**es, select **Y**es.

Using the Macro Library Manager with Release 2.x

5. Type the Macro Library range, which is A1..C3, and press Enter. Once again, the macros are removed from the worksheet and saved up to the GENERAL.MLB file.

6. Select No to password-protect your files.

Once again, the macros disappear from the screen. Now the Format macro in the Macro Library file GENERAL will format a cell for Currency with 0 Decimal Places. Let's try it out. Enter the number 10 in cell A1 and press Alt-F. Sure enough, the number is formatted with Currency with 0 Decimal Places.

Removing a Macro Library from Memory

As mentioned earlier, you can have multiple Macro Library files loaded into memory at the same time. If you detach the Macro Library Manager, all the library files are removed; you can't have a Macro Library file in memory without having the Macro Library Manager attached. However, there may be times when you have two or three Macro Library files loaded, and you want to remove only one of the files from memory. We're going to remove the GENERAL Macro Library file so that you can see how to remove a Macro Library file from memory. We are only removing the Macro Library file, not the Macro Library Manager add-in. The add-in remains in memory until you detach it. Therefore, remember that you can remove Macro Library files from memory without removing the Macro Library Manager add-in.

To remove the GENERAL Macro Library file from memory, follow these steps:

1. Press Alt-F7 to invoke the Macro Library Manager menu, and select Remove.

2. The library files that are in memory appear under the prompt
   `Enter name of macro library to remove.`

   In this example, we have only the GENERAL Macro Library file. Press Enter to select GENERAL.

The GENERAL Macro Library file is removed from memory, and the \r and \f macros in that file no longer are available.

Loading a Macro Library into Memory

When you first load 1-2-3 and then attach the Macro Library Manager, no Macro Library files (GENERAL or any others you may have created) are loaded into memory. You have to load the library you want to work with.

In this chapter, we created only one Macro Library file, GENERAL, but you can have as many library files with different types of macros as you want or need. Depending on the amount of RAM (random-access memory) you have in your machine, you can have one or more of your Macro Libraries loaded at the same time. I recommend that you have one Macro Library file with all the macros you frequently use, and have that one file loaded in the Macro Library Manager; you may have trouble keeping track of macro names if you load multiple library files.

OOPS! It's very important to remember that if you have several library files loaded, none of the macros can have the same name. All the macros are seen as a single group of macros even though they are in different library files. You will get unexpected results if two macros in library files loaded into the Macro Library Manager have the same name.

To load the GENERAL Macro Library file into memory, follow these steps:

1. Press Alt-F7 to invoke the Macro Library Manager menu, and select Load.

2. The library files that are available appear under the prompt Enter name of Macro Library to load.

    We have only the GENERAL Macro Library file. Press Enter to select GENERAL.

The GENERAL Macro Library file, containing the \r and \f macros, is loaded into memory. Enter your initials into a cell and press Alt-R to run the \r macro; the initials are erased. If you have other Macro Library files to load, you simply go through the same procedure.

98

From Here...

In this chapter, you learned how to use the Macro Library Manager available in 1-2-3 Release 2.x. This tremendously useful tool enables you to run your macros with any worksheet without having to re-enter your macros in each worksheet.

Next, you learn about macros that perform multiple tasks at once.

Advancing Your Use of Macros

PART III

Creating Macros That Perform Multiple Tasks

CHAPTER 9

Easy 1-2-3 Macros

So far, we have been creating simple macros that perform a single task. We created macros to erase data in Chapter 3, to change column widths in Chapter 4, and to format cells in Chapter 5. In this chapter, we're going to explore macros that perform multiple tasks.

When 1-2-3 runs a macro with multiple tasks stored in more than one cell, 1-2-3 reads the instructions in the first cell of the macro and activates the keys and commands in the order in which they appear in that label. Remember that all cells containing macro instructions are label cells. Macros stop when they encounter a blank cell or a number cell. After 1-2-3 processes all keys and commands in the first cell, it reads the cell located below that cell. If that cell contains a label, 1-2-3 also executes the macro instructions in that cell. This process continues until a nonlabel cell, usually a blank cell, is read. When this happens, 1-2-3 stops macro execution.

You probably will create many macros that perform several tasks for you. When you create macros that perform multiple tasks, you should use a separate line for each task. This process enables you to read and edit the macro easier.

A Macro That Enters Your Name and Address

In this example, we will create a macro that enters your name, address, city, state, and ZIP code.

First, let's identify the *manual* steps necessary to enter this information:

1. Type your name.
2. Move the cell pointer down one cell.
3. Type your address.
4. Move the cell pointer down one cell.
5. Type your city, state, and ZIP code.
6. Press Enter.

The preceding steps are the steps we need to tell the macro to perform.

Now we will begin to enter the macro. But first, you should know that the command to move the cell pointer down one cell is {D} (the letter *D* within curly braces). This macro key name presses the down-arrow key

Creating Macros That Perform Multiple Tasks

once. A macro key name performs a keyboard action such as {R} for Right, which presses the right-arrow key, or {BS} for Backspace.

OOPS! You must enter the {D} macro key name with curly braces and no spaces. The macro will produce an error if you don't enter this information correctly. (It doesn't matter whether you type a lowercase or uppercase D.)

Retrieve the LAYOUT worksheet and save the file with the name ADDRESS. To begin entering the macro, follow these steps:

1. Move the cell pointer to cell AB3.

2. Type your name followed by the {D} command, and press Enter.

   I will type **Don Roche Jr.{D}** and press Enter.

   The {D} after my name enters my name into the cell and then moves the cell pointer down one cell. Notice that there is no space between my name and the {D} command.

3. Move the cell pointer to cell AB4.

4. Type your address followed by the {D} command, and press Enter.

   I will type **"56 Creelmand Drive{D}** and press Enter.

5. Move the cell pointer to cell AB5.

6. Type your city, state, and ZIP code. Then press Enter.

   I will type **Fishers, IN 46038~** and press Enter.

This macro contains three lines that do the following: type your name into one cell; move the cell pointer down to the cell below that cell; type your address; move the cell pointer down to the cell below that cell; and type your city, state, and ZIP code.

Now we must name and document the macro. Follow these steps:

1. To name the macro, move the cell pointer to cell AA3.

2. Type **'\n** and press Enter.

3. Select **/R**ange **N**ame **L**abels **R**ight and press Enter.

4. To document the macro, move the cell pointer to cell AC3.

105

> **NOTE**
>
> If your address begins with a number, you must precede your address with a single quote ( ) before you enter your address in the cell. In addition, the macro requires *another* single quote before your address so that the macro actually types a single quote when it is run.
>
> For example, my address should appear as 56 Creelmand Drive{D} in the cell; this means I have to type *two* single quotes ("56 Creelmand Drive{D}) to enter the address in the cell. (This isn't a double quote. It's two single quotes typed one after another.)

5. Type **Macro to type in name, address, city, state, and zip** and press **Enter**.

Figure 9.1 shows the completed macro.

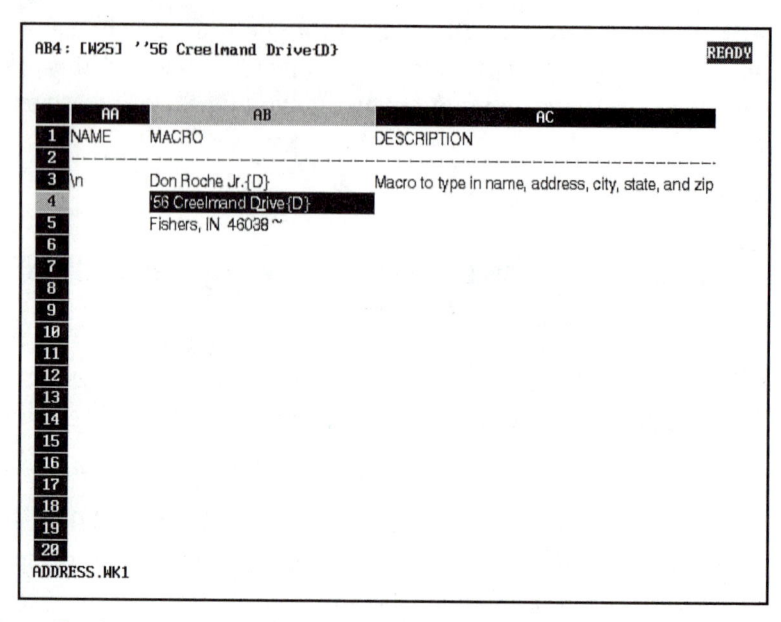

Fig. 9.1 The completed \n macro.

Now, let's run the macro. Move the cell pointer to cell A1 and press **Alt**-**N**. Your name is typed into cell A1, your address is typed into cell A2, and your city, state, and ZIP code are typed into cell A3. Figure 9.2 shows the results of running my \n macro.

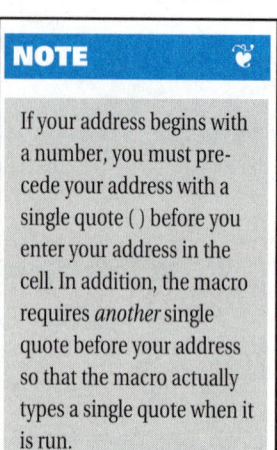

Creating Macros That Perform Multiple Tasks

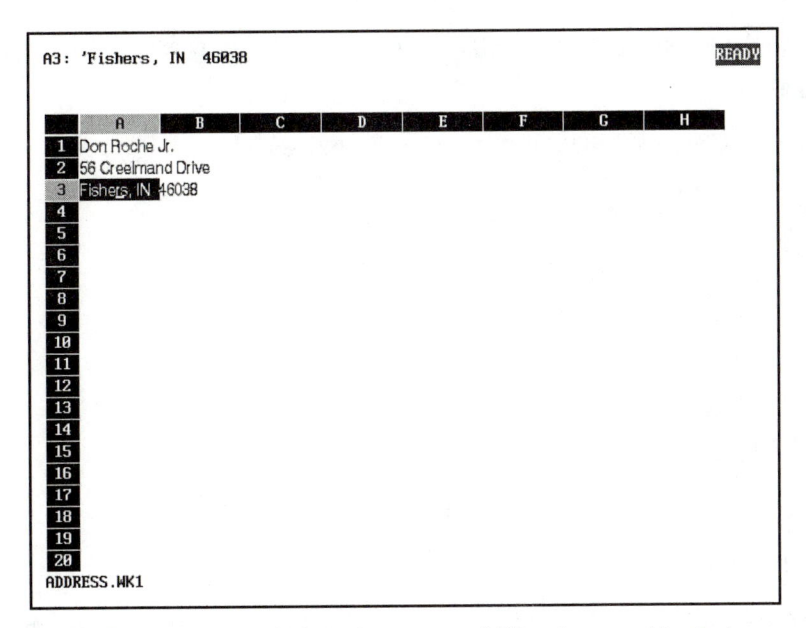

Fig. 9.2 The name, address, city, state, and ZIP code entered by the \n macro.

The macro executed the commands in column AB until it ran into the first blank cell—cell AB6 in this example.

Great! You have created your first multiple-task macro! Next, we'll create a macro that prints a worksheet with a footer.

A Macro That Prints a Worksheet with a Footer and Page Number

Many times, you want a footer to be on each page of your printout. We will create a multiple-task macro that prints a worksheet with a footer that includes the page number.

Retrieve the INCOME worksheet. The data area for this file is in the range A1..E12. This area will also be our print range. First, we need to write down the steps necessary to do this task.

Easy 1-2-3 Macros

To print a worksheet with a footer that includes the page number, follow these steps:

1. Press **/** to bring up the 1-2-3 main menu.
2. Select **P**rint.
3. Select **P**rinter.
4. Select **R**ange.
5. Define the print range and press **Enter**.
6. Select **O**ptions.
7. Select **F**ooter.
8. Type the footer information.
9. Print the worksheet.

The preceding are the steps you need to tell the macro to perform. Before you create the macro, erase any text or macros in the macro writing area (beginning in cell AA3).

Now you're ready to write the macro. To create the macro, follow these steps:

1. Move the cell pointer to cell AB3.
2. Type **'/pprA1..E12~** and press **Enter**.

   /pprA1..E12~ are the macro instructions to bring up the 1-2-3 main menu, select **P**rint, select **P**rinter, select **R**ange, type **A1..E12** as the print range, and press **Enter**.

3. Move the cell pointer to cell AB4.
4. Type **ofPage #~** and press **Enter**.

   ofPage #~ are the macro instructions to select **O**ptions, select **F**ooter, type **Page #** as the footer, and press **Enter**. The # is a special 1-2-3 convention that creates the correct page number for each page of the printout. You could include the date in your footer by typing the **@** symbol; @ is another special 1-2-3 convention.

5. Move the cell pointer to cell AB5.
6. Type **qagpq** and press **Enter**.

108

Creating Macros That Perform Multiple Tasks

QAGPQ are the macro instructions to select **Q**uit **A**lign **G**o **P**age **Q**uit. The first **Q**uit quits the **O**ptions menu; **A**lign correctly positions the paper for the printer; **G**o prints the range; **P**age advances the paper; and **Q**uit quits the **P**rint menu and returns 1-2-3 to READY mode.

Now we must name and document the macro. Follow these steps:

1. To name the macro, move the cell pointer to cell AA3.

2. Type **'\p** and press **Enter**.

3. Select **/R**ange **N**ame **L**abels **R**ight and press **Enter**.

4. To document each line of the macro, move the cell pointer to cell AC3.

5. Type **Enter the print range A1..E12** and press **Enter**. Then, type **Enter the footer Page #** in cell AC4, press **Enter**, and type **Print the range** in cell AC5.

Figure 9.3 shows the completed macro.

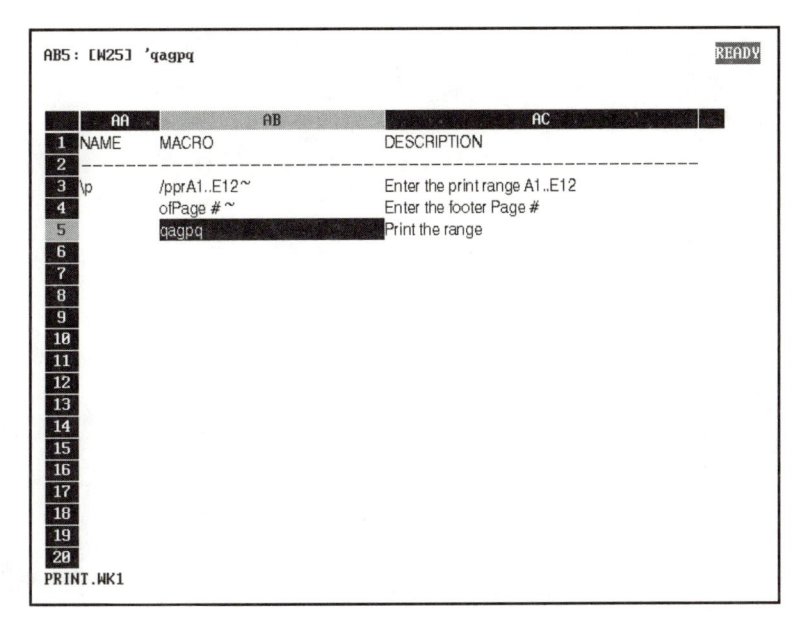

Fig. 9.3 The completed \p macro to print a range with a footer.

109

From Here...

You learned about multiple-task macros in this chapter. You created a macro to type your name, address, city, state, and ZIP code. You also created a multiple-task macro to print a worksheet with a footer.

Next, you will learn about some of the advanced macro commands. But don't worry—we won't get into anything too complicated!

Moving to the Next Level

CHAPTER 10

Easy 1-2-3 Macros

As we have learned, a macro, in it's simplest form, is a list of keystrokes and 1-2-3 commands. When the macro is executed, all the keys in the list are executed as though they are typed at the keyboard. A macro also can use special macro commands that provide enhanced capabilities for using and controlling 1-2-3. These commands are called *advanced macro commands*. (Don't let the word *advanced* scare you!)

The advanced macro commands offer you capabilities beyond simple keystroke emulation. You can control 1-2-3 with the advanced macro commands in ways that simply aren't available with keystroke recording.

What Are the Advanced Macro Commands?

The 1-2-3 advanced macro commands are a set of "invisible" commands. These commands are invisible because, unlike commands on the 1-2-3 menu (such as **/W**orksheet **C**olumn **S**et-Width), you cannot invoke the advanced macro commands from the keyboard. You can use these commands only in a macro. For example, the advanced macro command {BEEP} makes the computer beep. No menu command exists to make the computer beep.

Rules for the Advanced Macro Commands

You need to follow certain rules if you use the advanced macro commands. Some of these rules include the following:

♣ Each advanced macro command begins with an open curly brace ({) and ends with a close curly brace (}).

♣ Each advanced macro command has a *keyword* identifying the action to be taken. For example, the advanced macro command to end a macro immediately is:

   {QUIT}

Moving to the Next Level

> The macro keyword is typed immediately after the open curly brace in uppercase or lowercase. (In this book, macro keywords appear in uppercase.)

♣ Macro commands sometimes require additional information (called *arguments*) that 1-2-3 uses when executing the command. Arguments are included within the curly braces. (I know that *arguments* is an odd name, but it's the name Lotus has chosen.) A single space separates the keyword from the first argument. For example:

> {KEYWORD *argument*}

The following is another example of an argument:

> {RIGHT *5*}

RIGHT is the keyword, and *5* is the argument. This command instructs 1-2-3 to press the right-arrow key five times.

You can enter arguments in uppercase or lowercase. (In this book, arguments appear in lowercase.)

♣ Multiple arguments in an advanced macro command must be separated by commas, with no additional spaces. For example:

> {KEYWORD *argument1,argument2,...,argumentN*}

An example of multiple arguments is:

> {FOR *count,1,10,1,routine*}

FOR is the keyword and *count, 1, 10, 1* and *routine* are arguments. The preceding command instructs 1-2-3 to perform the macro instructions at routine ten times (starting at 1 and counting by 1 to 10).

♣ The entire advanced macro command must be entered in a single cell, not split between two or more cells.

Figure 10.1 shows examples of advanced macro commands entered correctly and incorrectly, respectively.

113

Easy 1-2-3 Macros

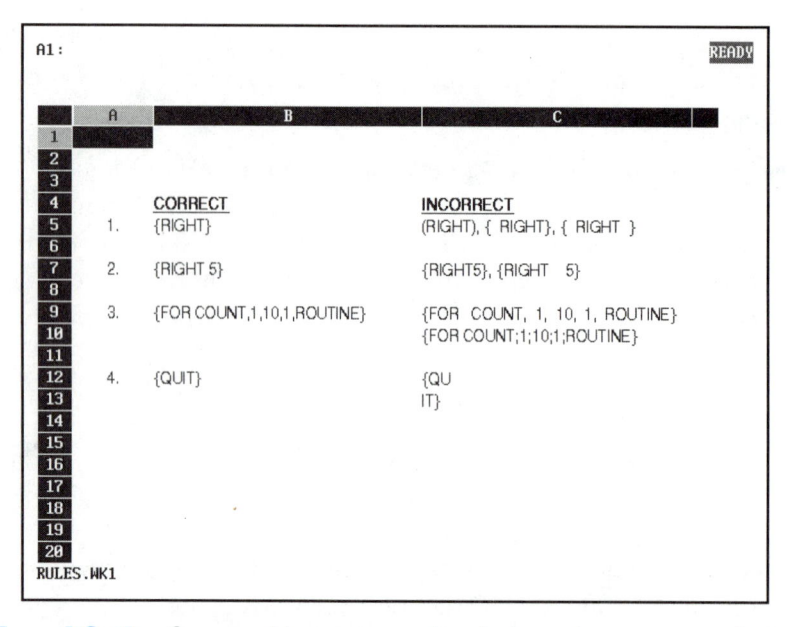

```
A1:                                                    READY
         A           B                    C
  1
  2
  3
  4              CORRECT              INCORRECT
  5        1.   {RIGHT}               (RIGHT), { RIGHT}, { RIGHT }
  6
  7        2.   {RIGHT 5}             {RIGHT5}, {RIGHT   5}
  8
  9        3.   {FOR COUNT,1,10,1,ROUTINE}   {FOR  COUNT, 1, 10, 1, ROUTINE}
 10                                          {FOR COUNT;1;10;1;ROUTINE}
 11
 12        4.   {QUIT}                {QU
 13                                   IT}
 14
 15
 16
 17
 18
 19
 20
RULES.WK1
```

Fig. 10.1 Correct and incorrect examples of advanced macro command rules.

The preceding list contains most of the rules you need to follow when using advanced macro commands. Keeping these rules in mind will save a lot of time and trouble.

You can get a complete list of keywords in the 1-2-3 documentation or on-line help. For on-line help, press **F1** and select **macros**.

From Here...

Now that we have learned a little about the advanced macro commands, we're ready to discuss some macros that use these commands.

In the next chapter, we will create an advanced macro command that pauses a macro until you press **Enter**. This advanced macro command is one of the most useful commands you will ever learn.

Pausing a Macro

CHAPTER 11

Easy 1-2-3 Macros

One of the most useful advanced macro commands is the command that pauses a macro. The pause command is indicated as {?}, a question mark within curly braces. The pause command has no arguments.

When a macro encounters a {?} command during macro execution, the macro pauses until you press **Enter**. This capability adds great flexibility to your macros since you can control the macro by pausing it for input. In this chapter, we create macros that pause to enable you to manually erase cells, format numbers, and widen columns. You may remember that we created macros (without the pause command) to accomplish each of these tasks in Chapters 3, 4, and 5.

Pausing a Macro To Erase Cells

There may be times when you don't know exactly which cells you want to erase. The {?} command gives you the flexibility to tell the macro which cells to erase by pausing for you to identify cell addresses.

Let's consider the macro we created in Chapter 3 to erase a cell—the /re~ macro. This macro enables you to erase the data in the current cell. If you don't move the cell pointer to the correct cell to erase the data *before* you run the macro, you're out of luck. A simple change to this macro enables you to tell the macro which cells you want to erase.

Retrieve the ERASE worksheet—the worksheet with the /re~ macro. Let's modify this macro so it pauses, enabling us to define the cell or range of cells we want to erase. The macro correctly erases the data at the correct cell pointer. You don't get a chance to tell the macro what cell or range of cells to erase because the **Enter** key is pressed immediately after **/**, **R**ange, and **E**rase are selected. Move the cell pointer to cell AB3. Edit the /re~ macro to read /re{?}~. You have just added the pause command to the /re macro by changing it to /re{?}. Now the macro pauses before pressing **Enter**. This pause enables you to identify the cell or range of cells to erase. Figure 11.1 shows the new macro. You can modify the description of this macro, as shown in figure 11.1.

Pausing a Macro

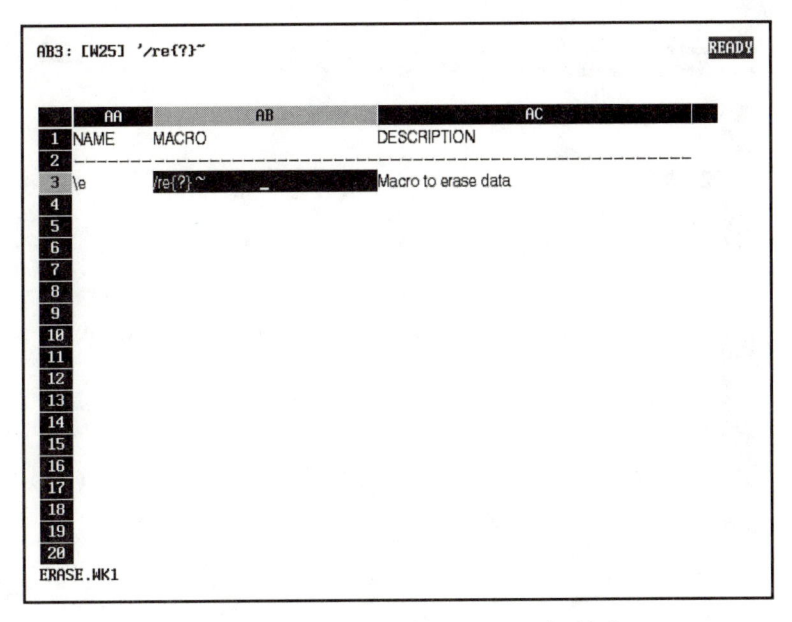

```
AB3: [W25] '/re{?}~                                    READY

        AA            AB                    AC
   1  NAME          MACRO              DESCRIPTION
   2  ----------------------------------------------------
   3  \e            /re{?}~    _       Macro to erase data
   4
   5
   ...
   20
ERASE.WK1
```

Fig. 11.1 The erase macro with a pause command added.

To use the erase macro with the pause command added, follow these steps:

1. Move the cell pointer to cell A1.

2. Enter your first name in cell A1, your middle initial in cell A2 (if you don't have one, make one up), and your last name in cell A3.

3. With the cell pointer in cell A3, press **Alt-E** to run the macro. (Remember, the \e macro name is unaffected by the change to the macro.)

The macro pauses after bringing up the 1-2-3 main menu and selecting **R**ange **E**rase. The CMD indicator is at the bottom of the screen. Remember that CMD indicates that you're running a macro. Figure 11.2 shows the paused macro. (The macro remains paused until you press **Enter**.)

Easy 1-2-3 Macros

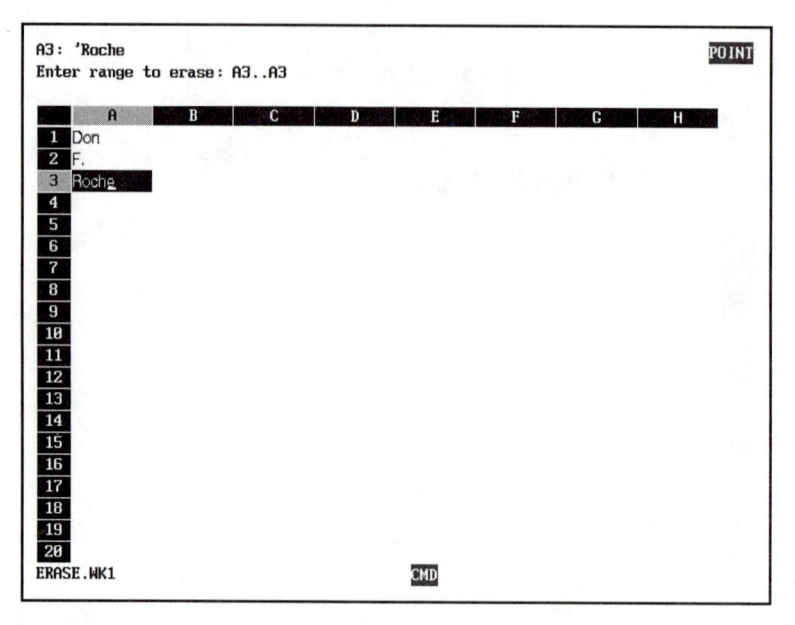

```
A3: 'Roche                                                    POINT
Enter range to erase: A3..A3

       A      B      C      D      E      F      G      H
  1  Don
  2  F.
  3  Roche
  4
  5
  ...
 20
ERASE.WK1                                      CMD
```

Fig. 11.2   The \e macro paused at the Enter range to erase: prompt.

4. Press the up-arrow key so the range in the prompt reads A3..A2, and press **Enter**.

   The labels in cell A2 and A3 are erased.

With this macro, you don't have to worry about the positioning of the cell pointer before you run the command. This macro is flexible because it pauses for you to highlight the cells to erase. But we can make it more flexible by unanchoring the cell pointer before we pause. What is *unanchor*? Well, I'm certainly not talking abut boats here. An anchored cell pointer appears as A3..A3. The two periods (..) in between the two cell addresses indicate that the cell pointer is anchored. An unanchored cell pointer appears as A3, simply the cell that the cell pointer is in. When you press an arrow key and the cell pointer is unanchored, the cell pointer moves in the arrow direction. For example, when you press **/P**rint **P**rinter **R**ange, the prompt at the top of the screen displays Enter print range: A1 (provided the cell pointer location was A1 when you chose **/ppr**). The cell pointer is unanchored. If you press the right-arrow key twice, the prompt becomes Enter print range: C1; you move the cell pointer to the right two cells.

118

Pausing a Macro

When you press an arrow key and the cell pointer is anchored, the cell pointer highlights in the arrow key direction. For example, when you press **/R**ange **E**rase, the prompt at the top of the screen displays `Enter range to erase: A1..A1` (provided that the cell pointer location was `A1` when you chose **/re**). The cell pointer is anchored. If you press the right arrow key twice, the prompt becomes `Enter range to erase: A1..C1`; you highlight the two cells to the right of `A1`.

If a cell pointer is anchored, you can unanchor it by pressing **Esc**. For example, if I choose **/R**ange **E**rase and the prompt appears as `Enter range to erase: A1..A1`, the prompt becomes `Enter range to erase: A1` when I press **Esc**. This action can be very handy if you haven't moved the cell pointer to the correct cell location before initiating the command.

OK, now that we know the difference between an anchored and an unanchored cell pointer, let's see how we can make our macro more flexible. When you select **/R**ange **E**rase, the cell pointer at the prompt is anchored. Therefore, if our macro unanchored the cell pointer before pausing, we can move the cell pointer to different cells to erase. We're not locked into highlighting cells from the location from which /re was executed by the macro.

The new macro would be /re{ESC}{?}~. As before, the macro pauses for you to identify the cell to erase; but now the cell pointer is unanchored so you can move it to a different cell location if necessary.

Pausing a Macro To Format Numbers

A macro that pauses so you can choose the format, the number of decimal places, and the range of cells to format is much more flexible and useful than a macro that simply formats a single cell with a predefined format and number of decimal places. We will edit the macro created in Chapter 5 to pause so we can specify which format we want to use and which cells we want to format.

Retrieve the FORMAT worksheet. Macro \d formats cells B6..E11 for Currency with 0 Decimal Places. Edit the /rfc~B6..E11~ macro to read /rf{?}~{?}~{?}~. Figure 11.3 shows the new macro. You can modify the description of this macro, as shown in figure 11.3.

> **NOTE**
>
> If you're erasing a range of cells, you can move the first cell, press the period key to anchor the cell pointer, and then use the arrow keys to highlight all the cells to erase.

119

Easy 1-2-3 Macros

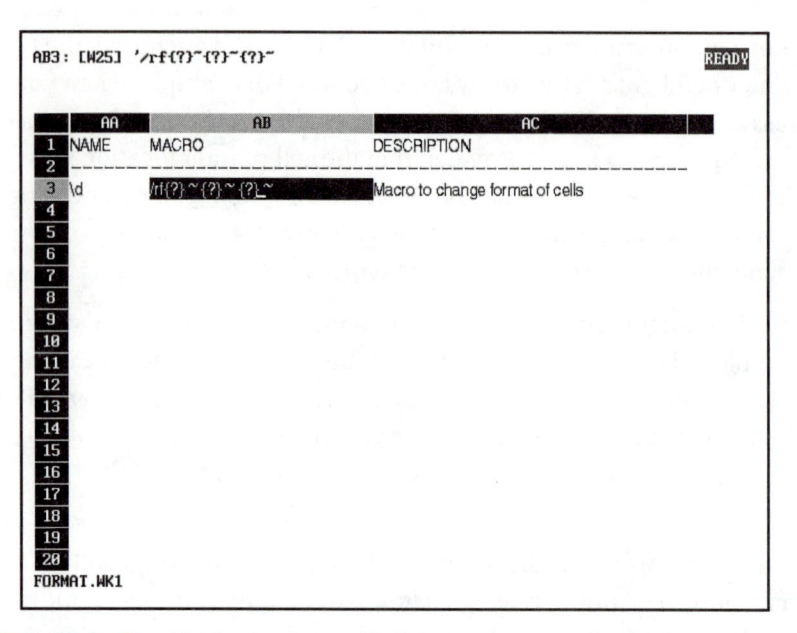

```
AB3: [W25] '/rf{?}~{?}~{?}~                                    READY

        AA              AB                        AC
  1  NAME          MACRO                DESCRIPTION
  2  --------------------------------------------------------
  3  \d            /rf{?}~{?}~{?}~      Macro to change format of cells
  4
  5
  6
  7
  8
  9
 10
 11
 12
 13
 14
 15
 16
 17
 18
 19
 20
FORMAT.WK1
```

Fig. 11.3 The format macro with three pause commands added.

To show you how you can use the format macro with three pause commands added, follow these steps:

1. Move the cell pointer to cell B6 and run the macro by pressing **Alt-D**.

   The macro pauses after bringing up the 1-2-3 main menu and selecting **R**ange **F**ormat. The CMD indicator at the bottom of the screen indicates that you're running a macro. Figure 11.4 shows the macro paused for the first pause command.

Pausing a Macro

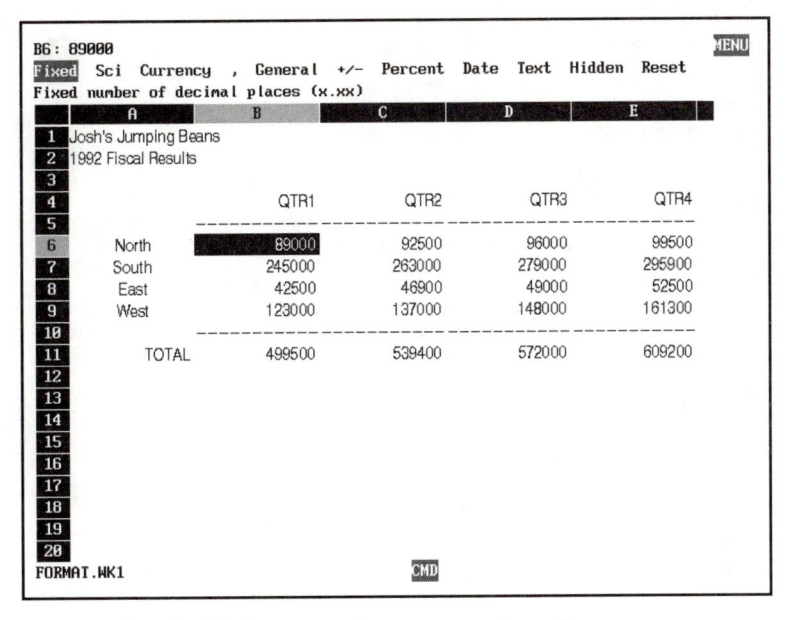

```
B6: 89000                                              MENU
Fixed  Sci  Currency  ,  General  +/-  Percent  Date  Text  Hidden  Reset
Fixed number of decimal places (x.xx)
         A           B           C           D           E
 1  Josh's Jumping Beans
 2  1992 Fiscal Results
 3
 4                  QTR1        QTR2        QTR3        QTR4
 5                  ---------------------------------------------
 6     North        89000       92500       96000       99500
 7     South       245000      263000      279000      295900
 8     East         42500       46900       49000       52500
 9     West        123000      137000      148000      161300
10                  ---------------------------------------------
11     TOTAL       499500      539400      572000      609200
12
...
20
FORMAT.WK1                      CMD
```

Fig. 11.4 The \f macro paused so you can select a format.

2. Highlight Currency and press Enter.

3. The macro then pauses to wait for you to enter the number of decimal places. Type 0 and press Enter.

4. The macro pauses again so you can highlight the range of cells to format. Press the down-arrow key three times so the specified range is B6..B9, and press Enter.

The macro ends, and the CMD indicator at the bottom of the screen turns off. Figure 11.5 shows the results.

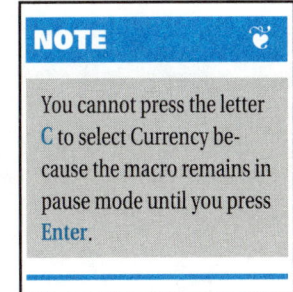

> **NOTE**
> You cannot press the letter C to select Currency because the macro remains in pause mode until you press Enter.

121

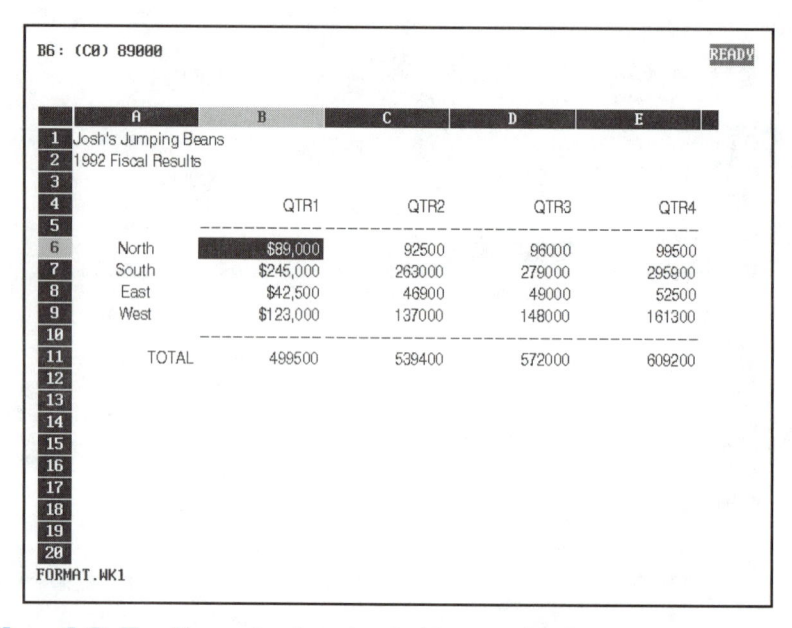

```
B6: (C0) 89000                                                READY

         A              B            C            D            E
 1  Josh's Jumping Beans
 2  1992 Fiscal Results
 3
 4                    QTR1         QTR2         QTR3         QTR4
 5                   --------------------------------------------
 6      North       $89,000       92500        96000        99500
 7      South      $245,000      263000       279000       295900
 8      East        $42,500       46900        49000        52500
 9      West       $123,000      137000       148000       161300
10                   --------------------------------------------
11      TOTAL       499500       539400       572000       609200
12
...
20
FORMAT.WK1
```

Fig. 11.5 The results of running the \f macro with three pause commands added.

You can also add the {ESC} command to your **/R**ange **F**ormat macro to make that macro more flexible. That macro would be /rf{?}~{?}~{ESC}{?}~. Again, the {ESC} command unanchors the cell pointer so you can position it.

Pausing a Macro To Change Column Widths

Column widths in a worksheet usually vary. One column may be fine with the default column width of 9, another column may need to be a width of 20, and another column may need to be a width of 28. Having a macro that changes the column width and pauses for you to enter the width is very useful. We're going to adapt one of the column-width macros we created in Chapter 4 so the macro pauses for you to enter the desired column width.

Pausing a Macro

Retrieve the COLUMN worksheet. Macro \w widens the current column to a width of 25. Edit the /wcs25~ macro to read /wcs{?}~. Figure 11.6 shows the new macro.

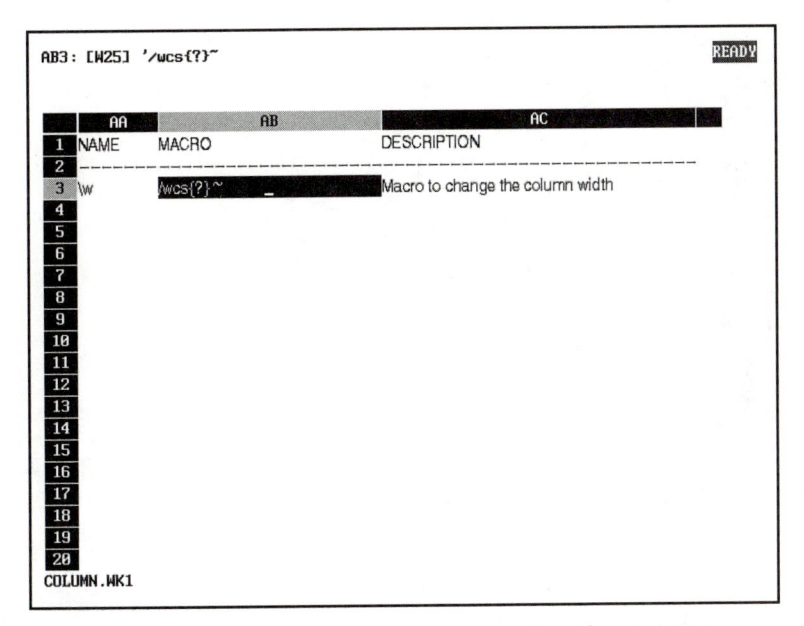

```
AB3: [W25] '/wcs{?}~                                          READY

           AA            AB                    AC
        1 NAME        MACRO              DESCRIPTION
        2 ----------------------------------------------
        3 \w          /wcs{?}~ _         Macro to change the column width
        4
        5
        6
        7
        8
        9
       10
       11
       12
       13
       14
       15
       16
       17
       18
       19
       20
       COLUMN.WK1
```

Fig. 11.6 The column width macro with the pause command added.

You can use the column width macro with the pause command added by following these steps:

1. Move the cell pointer to cell A1 and run the macro by pressing **Alt-W**.

   The macro pauses after bringing up the 1-2-3 main menu and selecting **W**orksheet **C**olumn **S**et-Width. The CMD indicator at the bottom of the screen indicates that you're running a macro. Figure 11.7 shows the paused macro.

123

Easy 1-2-3 Macros

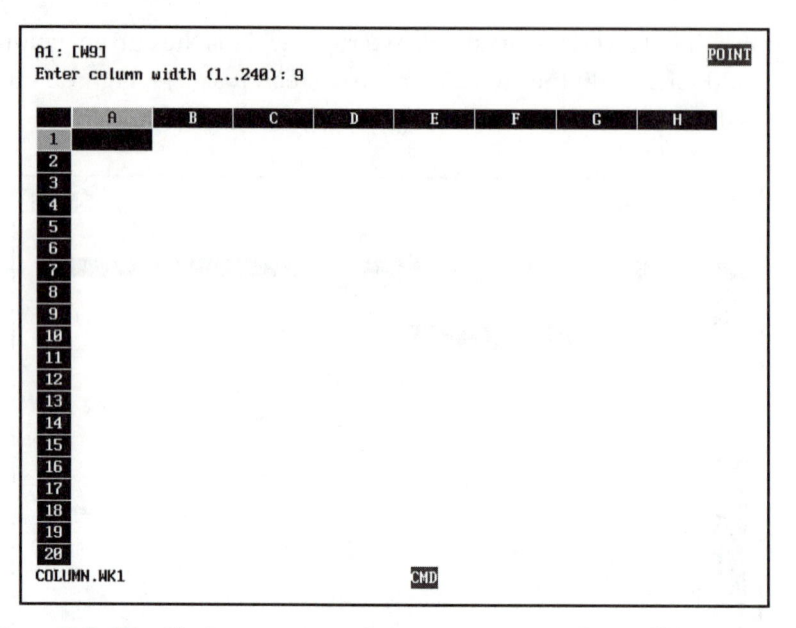

Fig. 11.7 The \w macro paused so you can enter a column width.

2. Type **35** and press **Enter**.

   When you press **Enter**, the macro ends and the C M D indicator at the bottom of the screen goes off. Figure 11.8 shows column A widened to 35.

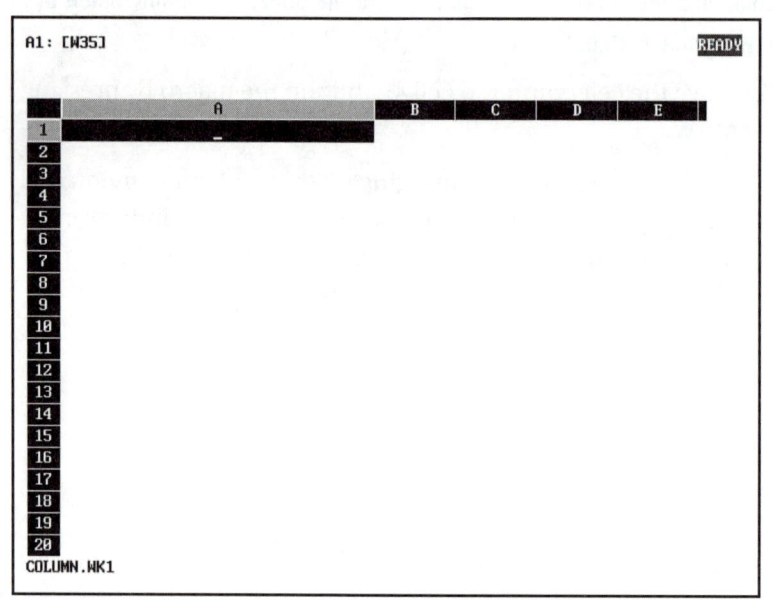

Fig. 11.8 The results of running the \w macro.

Pausing a Macro

You can move the cell pointer into any column and run this macro to change the column width to any width you need. This macro will come in very handy.

Creating a User Input Macro

An effective way to use the pause command is in a *user input macro*. With this type of macro, you move the cell pointer to a specific cell, pause for the user to enter something into the cell, move the cell pointer to the next cell, pause again, and so on. A user input macro can simplify the task of entering data.

The macro we create in this section is a multiple-line macro that performs several tasks. Retrieve the LAYOUT worksheet and save the worksheet with the name INPUT.

We first need to create some column headings for our data. Follow these steps:

1. Move the cell pointer to cell A1.

2. Enter the label **NAME** in cell A1, the label **DIVISION** in cell B1, and the label **SALARY** in cell C1. Then underline the labels.

3. Widen columns A, B, and C to 20.

4. Format column C for Currency with 0 Decimal Places. Your worksheet should resemble figure 11.9.

Easy 1-2-3 Macros

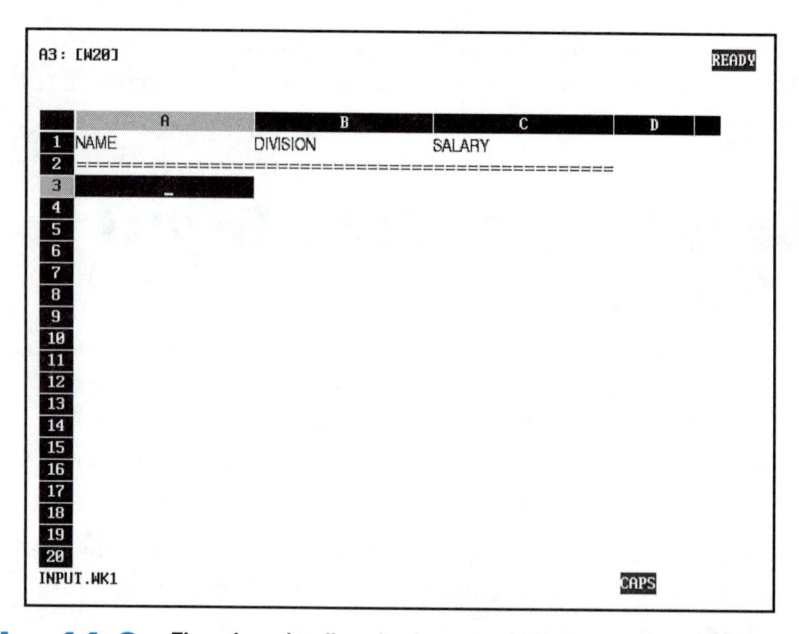

```
A3: [W20]                                                    READY
            A              B              C              D
    1  NAME           DIVISION       SALARY
    2  ========================================================
    3
    4
    5
    6
    7
    8
    9
   10
   11
   12
   13
   14
   15
   16
   17
   18
   19
   20
INPUT.WK1                                                    CAPS
```

Fig. 11.9 The column headings for data entered in the sample worksheet.

Before you begin writing your macro, I need to introduce another advanced macro command—the {BRANCH} command. The {BRANCH} command tells a macro to branch somewhere for instructions. We're going to use the {BRANCH} command to tell 1-2-3 to start our macro again by branching back to the first command of the macro. Sneaky, eh? This is called a *loop*. In a loop, the macro continues to execute until you tell it to stop by pressing **Ctrl-Break**. The {BRANCH} command needs one piece of information—where to branch (location). When you write a {BRANCH} command, you write it as follows:

{BRANCH *location*}

For example, you can write {BRANCH \e}, where \e is the name of a macro.

To create the user input macro, follow these steps:

1. Move the cell pointer to cell AB3.

2. Enter {HOME}{END}{D 2} into cell AB3.

126

Pausing a Macro

OOPS! The {D2} command must have a space between the D and the 2. This command instructs 1-2-3 to press the down-arrow key twice. The command will cause 1-2-3 to make an error during macro execution if you don't include the space.

OK, OK, I know you're asking yourself, "What the heck do the preceding commands do?" Well, I'm gonna tell ya. The {HOME} command moves the cell pointer to cell A1. The {END}{D 2} commands position the cell pointer correctly each time you run the macro to make sure you're not typing over any records already in the worksheet. The {D 2} command instructs 1-2-3 to press the down-arrow key twice. The first down-arrow key, pressed after the {END} command presses the END key, moves the cell pointer down to column A, to the last record. (Remember that the {HOME} command moved the cell pointer to cell A1.) Then the second down-arrow key moves the cell pointer directly below the last record, which is a blank row.

3. Once you position the cell pointer, you want the macro to pause so you can input a record. Enter {?}~{R} into cell AB4. The tilde (~) following the pause command {?} enters the data into the cell.

4. Next, you want the macro to move to the right one cell and pause again. Enter {?}~{R} into cell AB5.

5. You want the macro to once again move to the right one cell and then pause again. Enter {?}~ into cell AB6.

6. At this point, you want to loop back to begin the macro again. We loop back by using the {BRANCH} command. Enter {BRANCH \i} into the macro. You're going to name the macro \i, so you want to branch back to \i.

The macro is complete! Figure 11.10 shows the macro instructions.

Easy 1-2-3 Macros

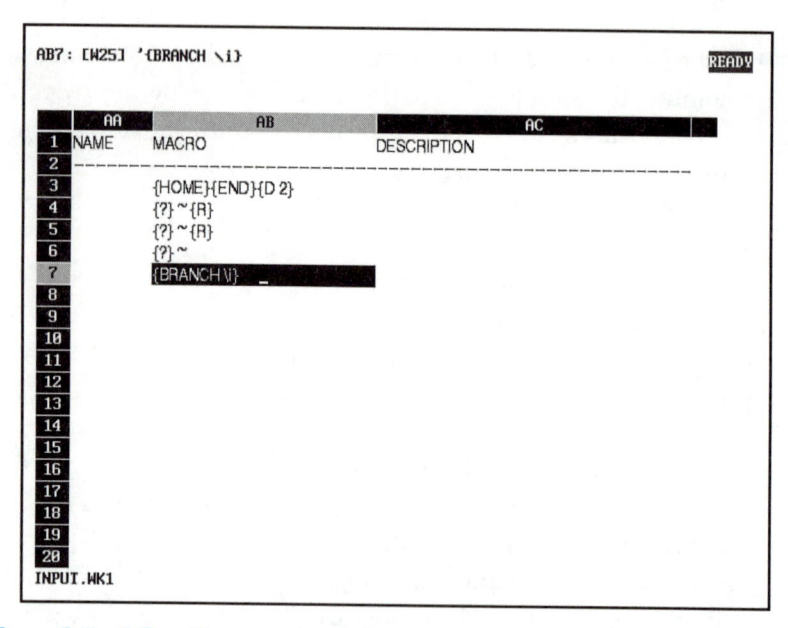

```
AB7: [W25] '{BRANCH \i}                                    READY

        AA            AB                      AC
  1  NAME         MACRO                DESCRIPTION
  2  --------------------------------------------------------
  3               {HOME}{END}{D 2}
  4               {?}~{R}
  5               {?}~{R}
  6               {?}~
  7               {BRANCH \i}   _
  8
  9
 10
 11
 12
 13
 14
 15
 16
 17
 18
 19
 20
INPUT.WK1
```

Fig. 11.10   The macro instructions for the user input macro.

Now we must name and document the macro. Follow these steps:

1. To name the macro, first move the cell pointer to cell AA3.

2. Type '\i and press Enter.

3. Select /Range Name Labels Right and press Enter.

4. To document the macro, move the cell pointer to cell AC3.

5. Type Position the cell pointer to enter record and press Enter. Then enter in cell AC4 Pause, enter Name, move cell pointer right; enter in cell AC5 Pause, enter Division move cell pointer right; enter in cell AC6 Pause enter Salary; and enter in cell AC7 Branch back to start again.

Your macro should now look like figure 11.11. Now, save the worksheet.

Pausing a Macro

```
AB3: [W25] '{HOME}{END}{D 2}                                      READY

      AA              AB                        AC
 1  NAME          MACRO                    DESCRIPTION
 2  ─────────────────────────────────────────────────────────
 3  \I            {HOME}{END}{D 2}         Position the cell pointer to enter record
 4                {?}~{R}                  Pause, enter Name, move cell pointer right
 5                {?}~{R}                  Pause, enter Division, move cell pointer right
 6                {?}~                     Pause, enter Salary
 7                {BRANCH \I}              Branch back to start again
 8
 9
10
11
12
13
14
15
16
17
18
19
20
INPUT.WK1
```

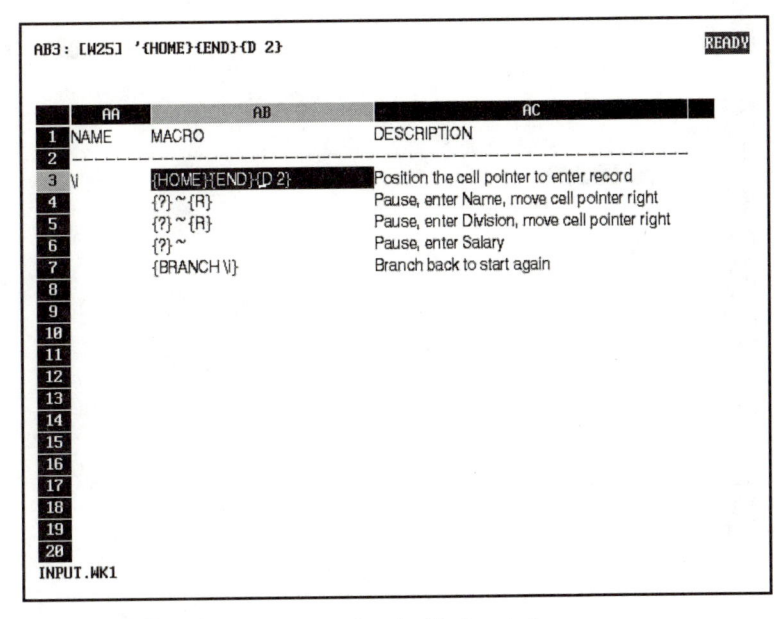

Fig. 11.11   The macro named and with descriptions.

To run the user input macro, follow these steps:

1. Press **Alt**-**I**.

   The cell pointer immediately moves to cell A3 and pauses. Row 3 is the first available row for inputting data because it has nothing in it. The CMD indicator at the bottom of the screen indicates that a macro is running. Figure 11.12 shows the cell pointer positioned for input.

129

Easy 1-2-3 Macros

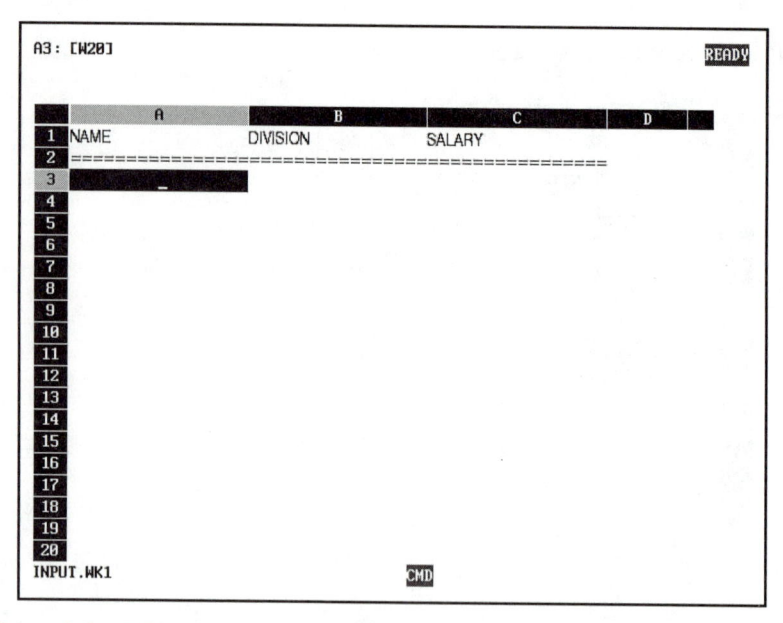

Fig. 11.12 The macro paused with the cell pointer in cell A3.

2. Type your name and press **Enter**.

    Your name is entered into cell A3, and the cell pointer is moved one cell to the right.

3. Type your division and press **Enter**.

    Your division is entered into cell B3, and the cell pointer is moved one cell to the right.

4. Type your salary and press **Enter**.

    Your salary is entered into cell C3, and the cell pointer is repositioned for the next record.

Figure 11.13 shows the completed entry and the repositioned cell pointer.

Pausing a Macro

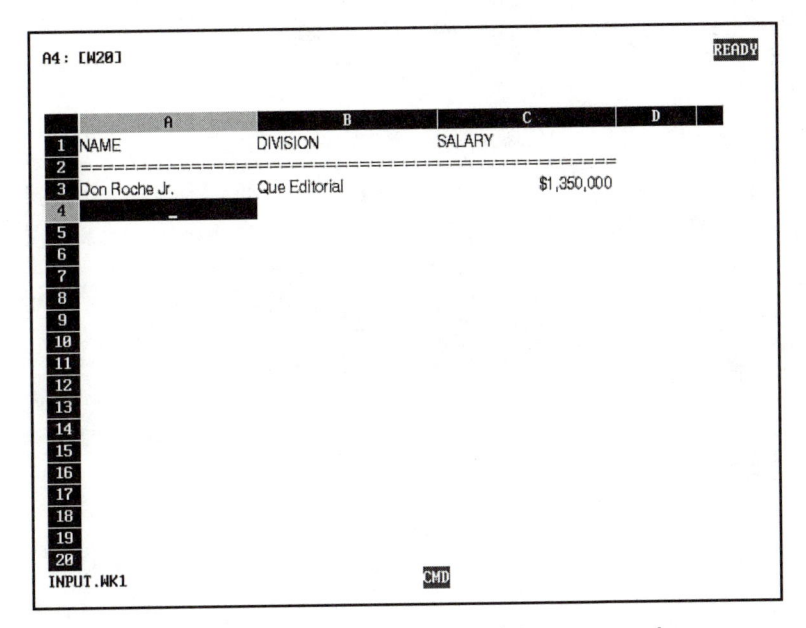

```
A4: [W20]                                              READY

        A               B                C           D
    1 NAME            DIVISION         SALARY
    2 ==================================================
    3 Don Roche Jr.   Que Editorial    $1,350,000
    4 _
    5
    6
    ...
   20
   INPUT.WK1                    CMD
```

Fig. 11.13   A record entered with the user input macro running.

By the way, I really don't make $1.35 million a year—I only make $1.2 million a year. (Yeah, right.)

The cell pointer is repositioned because the very first macro command was run again due to the {BRANCH \i} command. We looped back to start the macro again. (This macro will continue to run until you press **Ctrl-Break**.) Enter another record, and we'll stop the macro by pressing **Ctrl-Break**.

Figure 11.14 shows the error message that results. Press **Enter** or **Esc** to get out of ERROR mode and back to READY mode. When you return to READY mode, the macro stops. (Note that the CMD indicator at the bottom of the screen is turned off.)

Easy 1-2-3 Macros

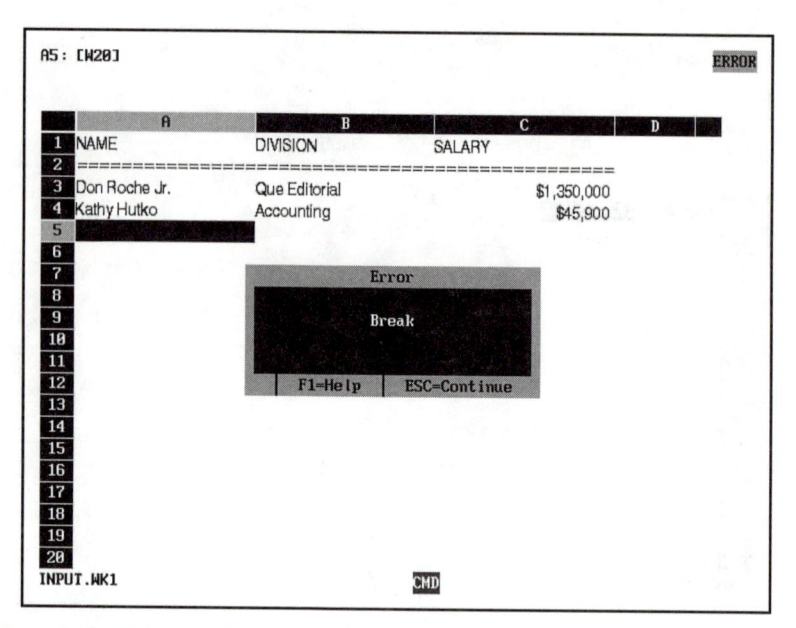

Fig. 11.14 The Ctrl-Break error message.

Now, to prove that the macro correctly positions the cell pointer for input, we will run the macro again. First, move the cell pointer to cell A1 by pressing the Home key. Then press Alt-I. Sure enough, as seen in figure 11.15, the cell pointer jumps to cell A5 and pauses for you to input a name.

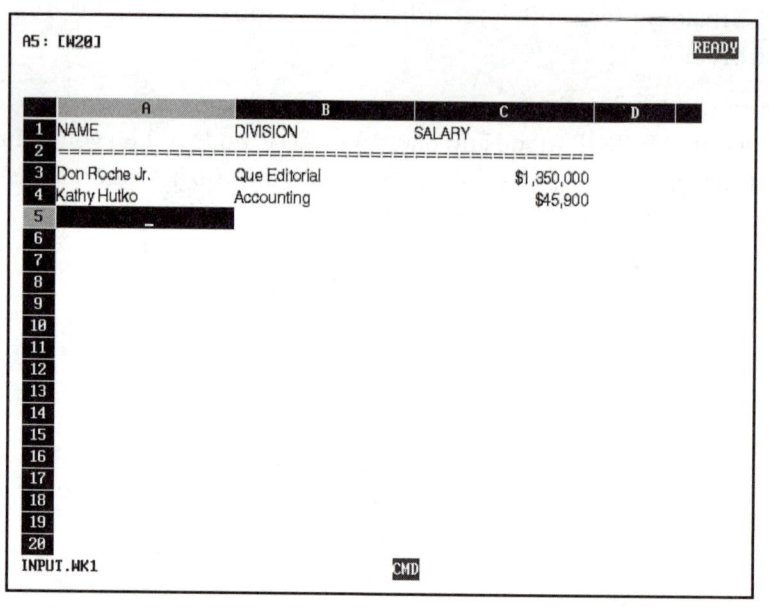

Fig. 11.15 The cell pointer correctly positioned for input.

From Here...

In this chapter, you learned about the pause macro {?} command. You learned that the {?} command pauses macro execution until you press Enter. This command enables your macros to be more flexible. You also learned how to create a user input macro by using the pause command.

Next, we will take a look at using a command that enables us to prompt the user for input.

Prompting the User for Input

CHAPTER 12

Easy 1-2-3 Macros

In the last chapter, we wrote a user input macro. The macro used the pause {?} command to pause macro execution so that the user could input a name, a division, or a salary. As you remember, the only way to stop that macro was to press **Ctrl-Break**. This is kind of a clunky way to stop a macro.

In this chapter, you learn how to stop a macro by having the macro ask you whether you want to stop. The macro actually prompts you to see if you want to continue. If you answer **Y**es by typing an uppercase **Y**, the macro continues. If you answer **N**o by typing an uppercase **N**, the macro quits.

Modifying the User Input Macro

First, we need to retrieve the INPUT worksheet from Chapter 11. You will add to this macro the steps necessary for the macro to query you as to whether you want to continue adding records or to quit. Figure 12.1 shows the INPUT worksheet.

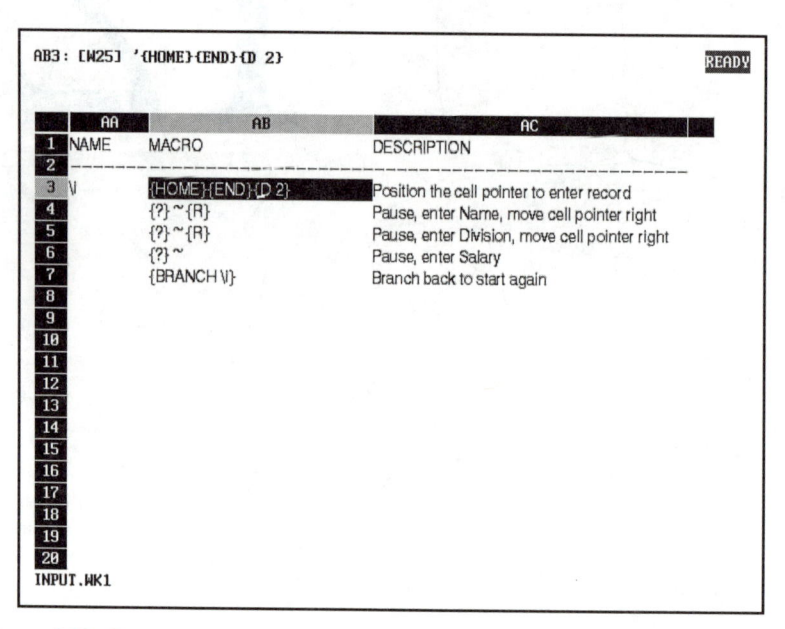

Fig. 12.1 The INPUT worksheet.

The first macro cell instruction correctly positions the cell pointer for a new record. The second and third macro cell instructions pause the

136

Prompting the User for Input

macro for input (name and division, respectively), and then move the cell pointer to the right one cell. The fourth macro cell instruction pauses the macro so that you can enter a salary. The last macro instruction, the {BRANCH \i} command, branches the macro back to \i, the first macro cell instruction, and begins the macro again. The only way to stop the macro is to press **Ctrl**-**Break**.

Understanding the {GETLABEL} Command

We're going to add a few more lines to the INPUT worksheet macro to make it a much better macro. First, you need to learn about two more advanced macro commands: {GETLABEL} and {IF}. Let's talk about {GETLABEL} first. The {GETLABEL} command is a great command. It's the command you use to prompt a user for input. The syntax for the {GETLABEL} command follows:

{GETLABEL "*prompt*",*location*}

For example, you can use the following command line:

{GETLABEL "What is your name? ",A1}

This example tells 1-2-3 to place the prompt `What is your name?` at the top of the screen. Whatever you type to answer the prompt is placed in cell A1, the *location* for {GETLABEL}. If you type **Tyler** when the prompt `What is your name?` appears, `Tyler` is placed in cell A1. If you type **Joshua Paul Roche** when the prompt appears, `Joshua Paul Roche` is placed in cell A1.

OOPS! It's very important to remember a few rules when using the {GETLABEL} command. First, there must be a space after the word GETLABEL. Second, the *prompt* argument must be in quotes. 1-2-3 doesn't care what prompt you use. For example, the prompt in the following statement is acceptable:

{GETLABEL "Yowza wowza, hgowza",A1}

You cannot include spaces before or after the comma separating the prompt from the *location* argument.

As you may know, everything in a 1-2-3 worksheet is considered a *value* (numbers or formulas) or a *label*. So, if you look at the word

137

{GETLABEL}, what the command *does* makes sense: It "gets" a label by prompting you for it and then storing it somewhere.

Understanding the {IF} Command

Many times, an {IF} statement is used to test what was typed in response to the {GETLABEL} prompt. In the following command, for example, what you type in response to the prompt `What is your name?` is placed in cell A1:

    {GETLABEL What is your name? ,A1}

The {IF} command then can test to see what is in cell A1. The general syntax for an {IF} command is:

    {IF statement} {True} {False}

The IF statement instructs 1-2-3 to perform the True macro instructions if the IF statement is True, and perform the False macro instructions if the IF statement is False.

The {IF} command works as follows:

    {IF A1=Tyler}{BRANCH \i}
    {QUIT}

This example is telling 1-2-3 to branch to \i if the name `Tyler` is in cell A1. If the name `Tyler` isn't in cell A1, quit the macro. So, the {IF} command checks to see what is in cell A1. If A1 contains the name `Tyler`, it does one thing. If A1 doesn't contain the name `Tyler`, it does something else.

How can you use this macro with a {GETLABEL} command? Well, if you add the {GETLABEL} command to the above example, you get the following:

    {GETLABEL What is your name? ,A1}
    {IF A1=Tyler}{BRANCH \i}
    {QUIT}

The {GETLABEL} command prompts you for a name. Whatever is typed in response to the prompt `What is your name?` is placed in cell A1. The {IF} command then tests to see what is in cell A1. If the name `Tyler` is in cell A1, the macro then branches to \i. If the name `Tyler` isn't in cell A1, the macro quits. This is the exact same kind of sequence we're going to use in our input macro.

Prompting the User for Input

Creating and Running the Macro

Let's write the new commands for our macro. First, we must erase cells AB7..AC7. We aren't automatically going to branch back to \i anymore, so we need to erase these commands.

Follow these steps:

1. Move the cell pointer to cell AB7 (if it's not already there).

2. Type **{GETLABEL "Enter another record? (Y/N) ",AB15}** and press **Enter**.

   The {GETLABEL} command prompts to see if the user wants to enter another record. The user will type an uppercase **Y** or an uppercase **N**, and then the macro continues or quits based on what the user types.

3. Move the cell pointer to cell AB8.

4. Type **{IF AB15="Y"}{BRANCH \i}** and press **Enter**.

5. Move the cell pointer to cell AB9.

6. Type **{QUIT}** and press **Enter**.

These commands tell 1-2-3 to branch to \i if Y is in cell AB15, or to quit the macro if Y is *not* in cell AB15.

The macro is already named, but we must add documentation to the last two macro cell instructions. Follow these steps:

1. Move the cell pointer to cell AB7.

2. Type **Prompt to continue or quit** and press **Enter**.

3. Move the cell pointer to cell AB8.

4. Type **If "Y", then continue** and press **Enter**.

5. Move the cell pointer to cell AB9.

6. Type **If not "Y", quit** and press **Enter**.

7. Also, for the sake of clarity, move to cell AA15 and enter the label **ANSWER**. This will identify what is entered into cell AB15 as the answer to the prompt.

Figure 12.2 shows the completed macro.

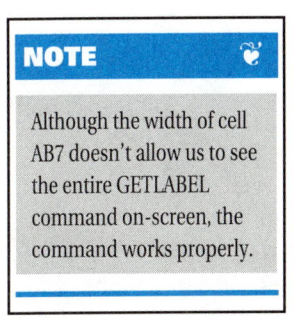

> **NOTE**
>
> Although the width of cell AB7 doesn't allow us to see the entire GETLABEL command on-screen, the command works properly.

139

Easy 1-2-3 Macros

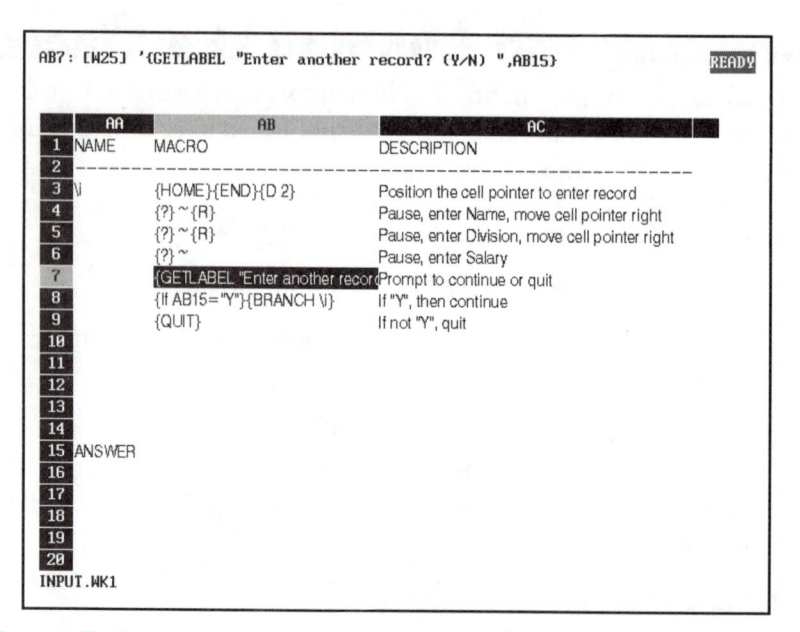

```
AB7: [W25] '{GETLABEL "Enter another record? (Y/N) ",AB15}        READY

       AA           AB                      AC
  1  NAME         MACRO                   DESCRIPTION
  2  ------------------------------------------------------------
  3  \i           {HOME}{END}{D 2}        Position the cell pointer to enter record
  4               {?}~{R}                 Pause, enter Name, move cell pointer right
  5               {?}~{R}                 Pause, enter Division, move cell pointer right
  6               {?}~                    Pause, enter Salary
  7               {GETLABEL "Enter another record  Prompt to continue or quit
  8               {If AB15="Y"}{BRANCH \i}  If "Y", then continue
  9               {QUIT}                  If not "Y", quit
 10
 11
 12
 13
 14
 15  ANSWER
 16
 17
 18
 19
 20
INPUT.WK1
```

Fig. 12.2 The completed macro with the {GETLABEL} and {IF} commands.

To run the macro, follow these steps:

1. Press **Alt-I**.

   The macro executes the first command, which positions the cell pointer at the next blank row in our database. This row is row 5 because we entered two records into rows 3 and 4 when we ran the macro in Chapter 11.

2. Enter a name, division, and salary.

   As soon as you enter a salary, the following prompt appears:

   ```
   Enter another record? (Y/N)
   ```

   This is the {GETLABEL} prompt (see fig. 12.3).

140

Prompting the User for Input

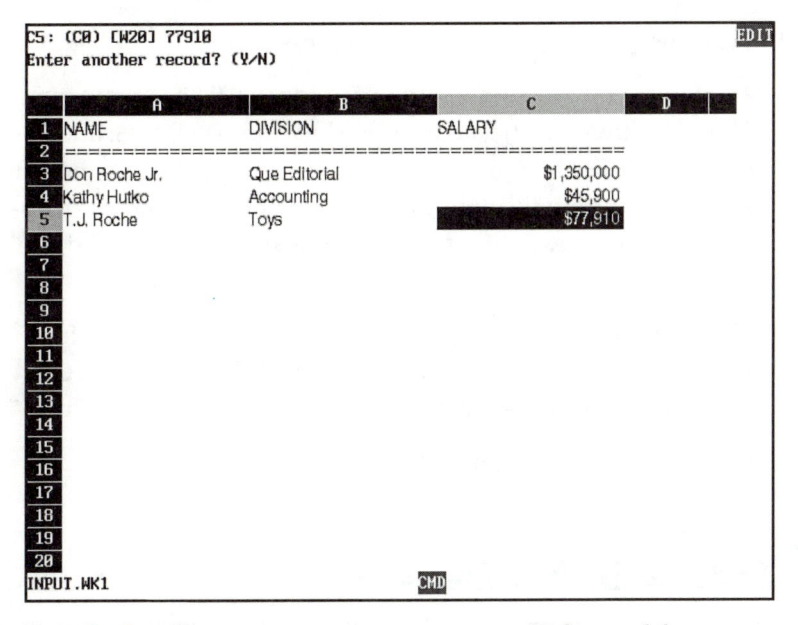

```
C5: (C0) [W20] 77910                                          EDIT
Enter another record? (Y/N)
        A                B                  C              D
 1  NAME            DIVISION           SALARY
 2  =====================================================
 3  Don Roche Jr.   Que Editorial         $1,350,000
 4  Kathy Hutko     Accounting               $45,900
 5  T.J. Roche      Toys                     $77,910
 6
 7
 8
 9
10
11
12
13
14
15
16
17
18
19
20
INPUT.WK1                         CMD
```

Fig. 12.3 The {GETLABEL} prompt appears at the top of the screen.

3. Type an uppercase **Y** and press **Enter**.

OOPS! You must type an uppercase **Y** because we're only testing for an uppercase Y.

When you type the uppercase **Y** and press **Enter**, the macro continues by branching back to the beginning of the macro. The {IF} statement tests to see what is in cell AB15 (which is Y in this case, because you entered Y in response to the {GETLABEL} prompt). Because an uppercase Y is in cell AB15, the macro continues and the cell pointer is correctly positioned for the next record.

4. Enter another name, division, and salary.

Once again, as soon as you enter a salary, the prompt appears.

141

> **NOTE**
>
> You can make the macro more flexible by adding an @UPPER function to the {IF} command. This action allows an uppercase or lowercase Y to be acceptable. The {IF} command would change to {IF @UPPER (AB15)=Y}. The @UPPER evaluates what is in cell AB15 as uppercase so a lowercase y is tested as an uppercase Y for the {IF} command.

5. Type an uppercase **N** this time and press **Enter**.

   As soon as you press Enter after pressing the **N,** the macro quits. The {IF} statement checked to see what was in cell AB15, and because it was not an uppercase Y, the macro quit. The CMD indicator disappeared from the bottom of the screen. A CALC indicator appears; simply press **Enter** to recalculate the worksheet, and you're done.

   Although we are prompting for **Y** or **N,** we are only testing for **Y.** Because we are only testing for **Y,** any other letter typed at the prompt will cause the macro to quit.

Excellent! Save the worksheet as PROMPT.

From Here...

In this chapter, you learned how to create a macro that prompts a user for information—specifically, whether the user wants to continue entering records. You learned how to use the {IF} command and how to use it with the {GETLABEL} command.

You did some pretty high level work in this chapter. You've accomplished a lot!

Next we will look at using the {IF} command to test specific spreadsheet conditions.

Testing for Worksheet Conditions

CHAPTER 13

Easy 1-2-3 Macros

The {IF} command is an enormously useful command that enables you to control your macros. The capability to test your worksheet and then create different commands based on that test is crucial for many macros.

As you learned in Chapter 12, you use the {IF} command to test for worksheet conditions. The {IF} command tests something and makes a decision based on that test. In the preceding chapter, we used the {IF} command to test the user's response to the {GETLABEL} prompt.

In this chapter, you learn how to use greater than (>) and less than (<) operators to test values. We're also going to explore using @functions with the {IF} command to help test for worksheet conditions.

Using Operators with the {IF} Command

The {IF} command can test labels, numbers, or, as we will see in the next section, cell conditions. In the preceding chapter, we used the {IF} command to test a label. In this chapter, we will look at testing numbers. You can test for *equal to* number conditions or a *greater than* or *less than* number condition. The following {IF} command, for example, tells 1-2-3 to beep if cell B20 contains the number 15. If cell B20 doesn't contain the number 15, the macro quits:

```
{IF B20=15}{BEEP}
{QUIT}
```

Retrieve the LAYOUT worksheet. Save the worksheet with the name BONUS. Create the worksheet displayed in figure 13.1.

Testing for Worksheet Conditions

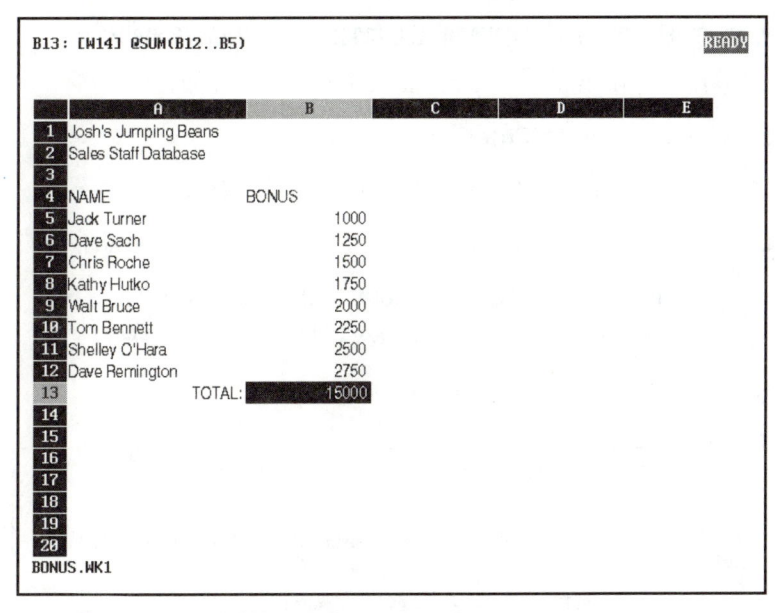

```
B13: [W14] @SUM(B12..B5)                                    READY

       A              B           C           D           E
 1  Josh's Jumping Beans
 2  Sales Staff Database
 3
 4  NAME           BONUS
 5  Jack Turner     1000
 6  Dave Sach       1250
 7  Chris Roche     1500
 8  Kathy Hutko     1750
 9  Walt Bruce      2000
10  Tom Bennett     2250
11  Shelley O'Hara  2500
12  Dave Remington  2750
13         TOTAL:  15000
14
15
16
17
18
19
20
BONUS.WK1
```

Fig. 13.1 The BONUS worksheet.

We're going to write a macro to change the format of the numbers to Currency with 0 Decimal Places. We're going to format the numbers only if the total of these numbers is greater than 20,000.

To create the macro, follow these steps:

1. Move the cell pointer to cell AB3.

2. Type **{IF B13<20000}{QUIT}** and press **Enter**.

   The preceding is an {IF} command to test whether the number in cell B13 is less than 20,000. If the number is less than 20,000, the macro quits.

3. Move the cell pointer to cell AB4.

4. Type **'/rfc2~B5..B12~** and press **Enter**.

   /rfc2~B5..B12 are the macro instructions to format the range B5..B12 to Currency with 2 Decimal Places. This command is run only if the number in cell B13 is *not* less then 20,000.

Easy 1-2-3 Macros

Now, we must name and document the macro. Follow these steps:

1. To name the macro, move the cell pointer to cell AA3.

2. Type **'\f** and press **Enter**.

3. Select **/R**ange **N**ame **L**abels **R**ight and press **Enter**.

4. To document the macro, move the cell pointer to cell AC3.

5. Type **Check Total; Quit if <20,000** and press **Enter**. Then type **Format cells B5..B12 to Currency 2 decimals** in cell AC4.

Figure 13.2 shows the completed macro.

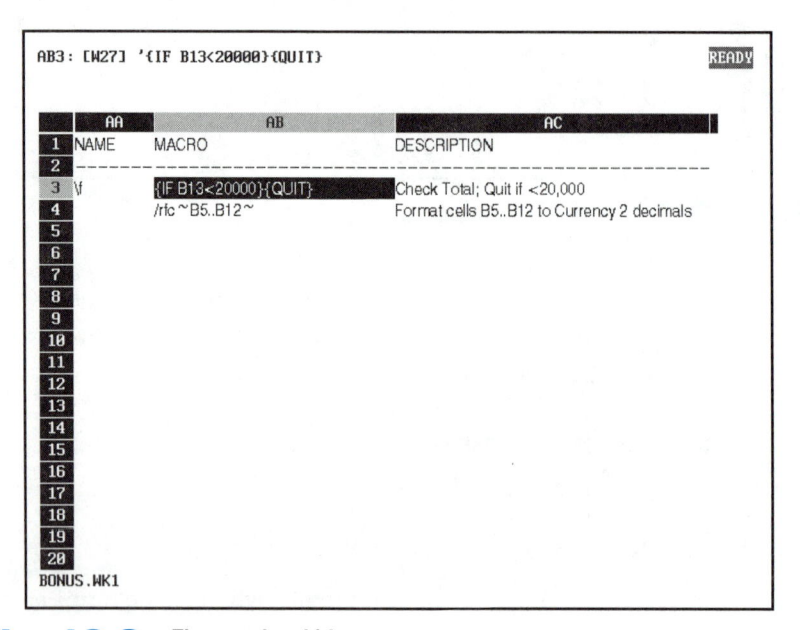

```
AB3: [W27] '{IF B13<20000}{QUIT}                                    READY

        AA              AB                          AC
  1   NAME            MACRO                    DESCRIPTION
  2   ------------------------------------------------------------------
  3   \f              {IF B13<20000}{QUIT}     Check Total; Quit if <20,000
  4                   /rfc~B5..B12~            Format cells B5..B12 to Currency 2 decimals
  5
  ...
 20
BONUS.WK1
```

Fig. 13.2 The completed \f macro.

Move the cell pointer back to cell A1 so we can watch the macro perform. The total in cell B13 is not greater than 20,000; therefore, the macro should not perform the format because it will quit immediately. Run the macro by pressing **Alt-F**. Sure enough, nothing is formatted.

Enter the number **10000** in cell B5. This changes the total in cell B13 to 24000. Now when we run the macro again, the numbers in cells B5..B12 are formatted to Currency with 2 Decimal Places (see fig. 13.3).

Testing for Worksheet Conditions

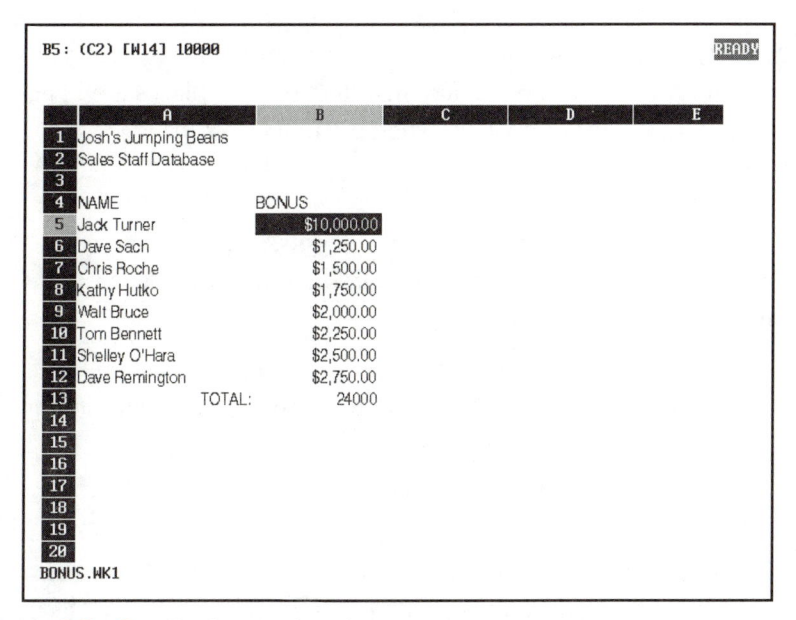

```
B5: (C2) [W14] 10000                                    READY

         A              B          C        D        E
  1  Josh's Jumping Beans
  2  Sales Staff Database
  3
  4  NAME            BONUS
  5  Jack Turner       $10,000.00
  6  Dave Sach          $1,250.00
  7  Chris Roche        $1,500.00
  8  Kathy Hutko        $1,750.00
  9  Walt Bruce         $2,000.00
 10  Tom Bennett        $2,250.00
 11  Shelley O'Hara     $2,500.00
 12  Dave Remington     $2,750.00
 13          TOTAL:       24000
 14
 15
 16
 17
 18
 19
 20
BONUS.WK1
```

Fig. 13.3 The formatted numbers.

The {IF} command is a very powerful command, and you will use it frequently when writing macros.

Using @CELLPOINTER with the {IF} Command

The @CELLPOINTER function is a very helpful function when using macros. The @CELLPOINTER function enables you to test for conditions at the current cell-pointer location. The following {IF} command, for example, tells 1-2-3 to beep if the current cell (remember, the *current* cell is always the one with the cell pointer) contains the number 10. If the current cell doesn't contain the number 10, the macro quits:

```
{IF @CELLPOINTER( contents )<>10}{BEEP}
{BEEP}
```

Note that the word *contents* is in quotes and has parentheses surrounding the quotes. Also note that @CELLPOINTER is one word. The word *contents* is a literal argument and must be entered exactly as shown. The {@CELLPOINTER} command is very flexible. You can test for the contents of a cell and for the cell's width, the cell's format, and other characteristics of the cell. Refer to your 1-2-3 manual for all the @CELLPOINTER attributes.

147

Easy 1-2-3 Macros

OOPS! There is only one space in the {IF} command, and that is directly after the keyword IF. Spaces inserted in other places aren't acceptable and will cause an error when the macro is run.

Because macros frequently move the cell pointer to different cells, it's very handy to be able to test for a condition at the current cell-pointer location.

The @CELLPOINTER command can test for a variety of factors. The following {IF} command tells 1-2-3 to quit if the current cell width isn't 20. If the current cell width is 20, the macro beeps:

```
{IF  @CELLPOINTER( width )<>20}{QUIT}
{BEEP}
```

You also can test for the format of a cell. The following {IF} command tells 1-2-3 to beep if the current cell format is Currency with 2 Decimal Places (which is represented by C2; if we were testing for Currency with 0 Decimal Places, we would substitute C0). If the current cell format isn't Currency with 2 Decimal Places, the macro quits; otherwise, it beeps:

```
{IF  @CELLPOINTER( format )<>C2}{QUIT}
{BEEP}
```

One of the most popular uses of the @CELLPOINTER function is @CELLPOINTER("type") to test for a blank cell. The following {IF} command tells 1-2-3 to quit if the current cell is blank. If the current cell isn't blank, the macro beeps:

```
{IF  @CELLPOINTER( type )= b }{QUIT}
{BEEP}
```

Note that the *b*, which represents *blank*, is in quotes.

Retrieve the BONUS worksheet and save the worksheet with the name SALES. Figure 13.4 shows a worksheet listing the sales staff for Josh's Jumping Beans. Be sure to change the worksheet shown in figure 13.3 so that the BONUS column is now the DIVISION column and enter the labels for the column. We're going to write a macro to center align the DIVISION labels. The macro will stop when it encounters a blank cell, which will be at the end of the list.

Testing for Worksheet Conditions

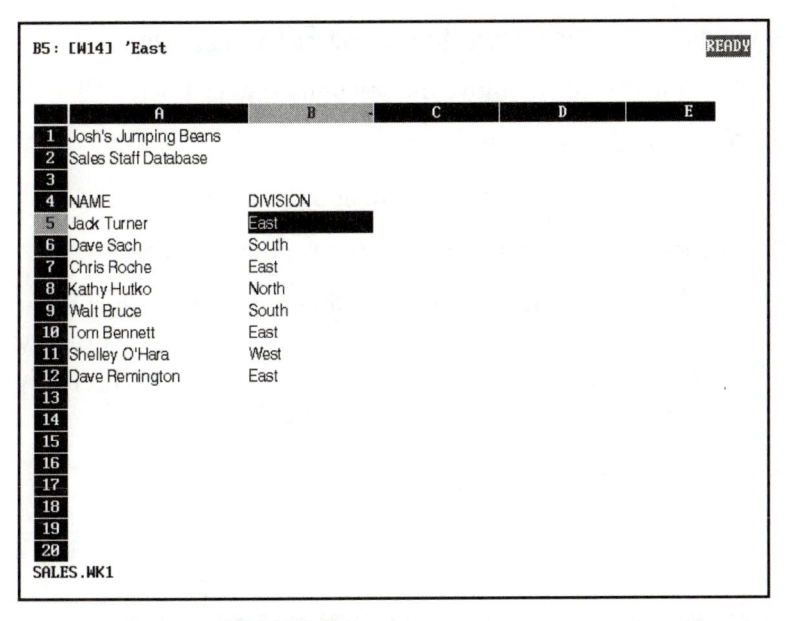

```
B5: [W14] 'East                                              READY

            A              B         C         D         E
    1  Josh's Jumping Beans
    2  Sales Staff Database
    3
    4  NAME           DIVISION
    5  Jack Turner    East
    6  Dave Sach      South
    7  Chris Roche    East
    8  Kathy Hutko    North
    9  Walt Bruce     South
   10  Tom Bennett    East
   11  Shelley O'Hara West
   12  Dave Remington East
   13
   14
   15
   16
   17
   18
   19
   20
SALES.WK1
```

Fig. 13.4   The SALES worksheet.

To create the macro to center align the DIVISION labels, follow these steps:

1. Move the cell pointer to cell AB3.

2. Type '/rlc~ and press Enter.

    /rlc~ are the macro instructions to change a label alignment to center.

3. Move the cell pointer to cell AB4.

4. Type {IF @CELLPOINTER("type")="b"}{QUIT} and press Enter.

    The {IF} command instructs 1-2-3 to quit if the current cell is blank.

5. Move the cell pointer to cell AB5.

6. Type {D} and press Enter.

    This macro command instructs 1-2-3 to move the cell pointer down one cell.

7. Move the cell pointer to cell AB6.

8. Type {BRANCH \l} and press Enter.

    This macro command instructs 1-2-3 to branch back and start the macro again, which means to align the next label.

149

Easy 1-2-3 Macros

Now we must name and document the macro. Follow these steps:

1. To name the macro, move the cell pointer to cell AA3.

2. Type **'\l** and press **Enter**.

3. Select **/R**ange **N**ame **L**abels **R**ight and press **Enter**.

4. To document the macro, move the cell pointer to cell AC3.

5. Type **Macro to center align a label** and press **Enter**. Then type **Test for blank cell; Quit if blank** in cell AC4, and press **Enter**. Type **Move the cell pointer down** in cell AC5, and press **Enter**. Finally, type **Branch to run the macro again** in cell AC6.

The completed macro appears in figure 13.5.

```
AB4: [W32] '{IF @CELLPOINTER("type")="b"}{QUIT}          READY

        AA          AB                          AC
 1    NAME        MACRO                       DESCRIPTION
 2    ---------------------------------------------------
 3    \l          /rlc~                       Macro to center align a label
 4                {IF @CELLPOINTER("type")="b"}{QUIT}  Test for blank cell; Quit if blank
 5                {D}                         Move the cell pointer down
 6                {BRANCH \l}                 Branch to run the macro again
 7
 8
...
20
SALES.WK1
```

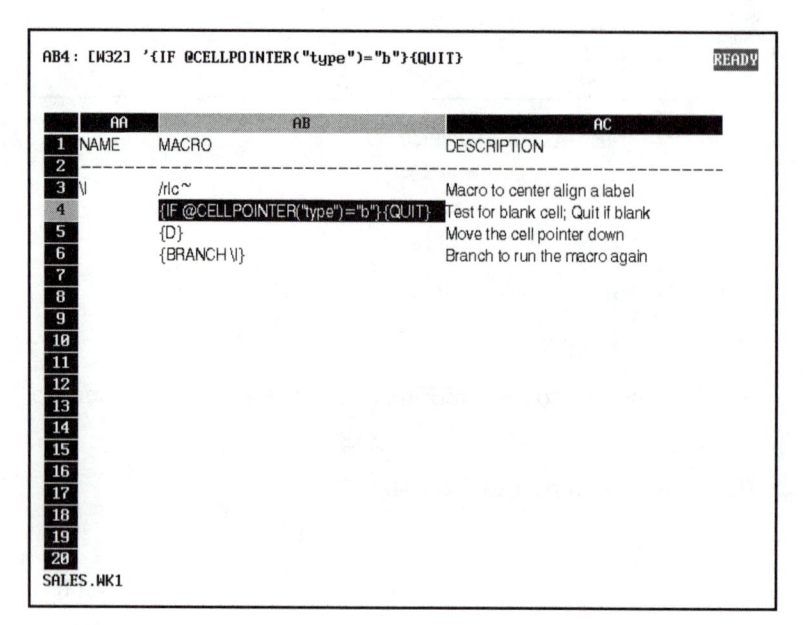

Fig. 13.5 The completed \l macro.

Move the cell pointer back to cell B5 and start the macro by pressing Alt-L. Figure 13.6 shows the result of running the \l macro.

150

Testing for Worksheet Conditions

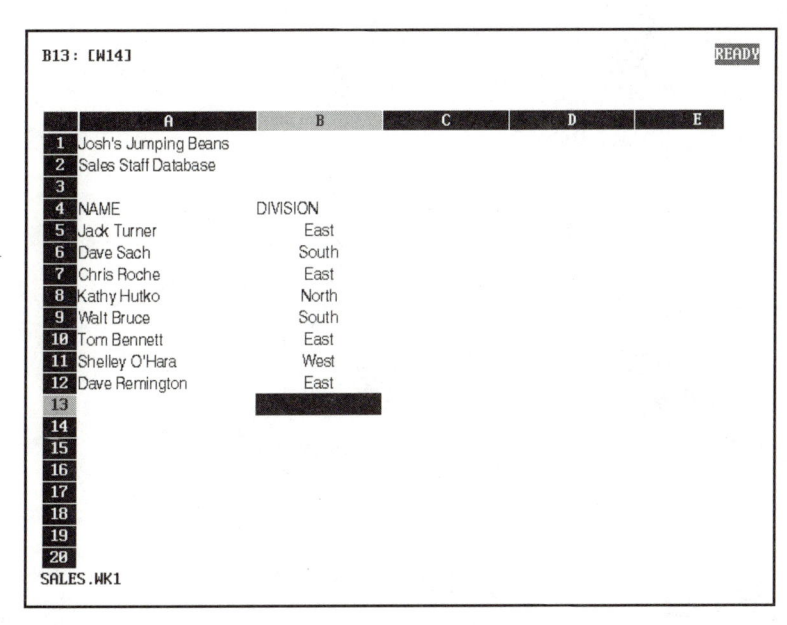

```
B13: [W14]                                                      READY

        A              B              C         D         E
   1  Josh's Jumping Beans
   2  Sales Staff Database
   3
   4  NAME           DIVISION
   5  Jack Turner    East
   6  Dave Sach      South
   7  Chris Roche    East
   8  Kathy Hutko    North
   9  Walt Bruce     South
  10  Tom Bennett    East
  11  Shelley O'Hara West
  12  Dave Remington East
  13
  14
  15
  16
  17
  18
  19
  20
SALES.WK1
```

Fig. 13.6   The macro changes the alignment of labels, centering them in column B.

The macro travels down the column of labels and changes each to a center aligned label. The macro stops as soon as a blank cell is encountered. The {IF} command tests each cell to see if the cell contains data. If the cell does contain data, the macro moves the cell pointer down one cell and branches back to start the macro again. If the cell does *not* contain data, the macro quits. Therefore, as soon as the macro reaches cell B13, the first blank cell in that column, it quits.

Testing for a blank cell by using the @CELLPOINTER("type")="b" function with an {IF} command is a very popular test to stop macro execution.

From Here...

In this chapter, you learned how to use the less than, greater than, and equal to operators with the {IF} command. You also learned how to use the @CELLPOINTER function with the {IF} command to test for various worksheet conditions.

Next, we will have some fun with the {BEEP} command.

Making the Computer Beep

CHAPTER 14

Easy 1-2-3 Macros

Every computer beeps. You probably have heard your computer beep when you have done something wrong. If you're using 1-2-3 right now, you can hear the beep by pressing the Backspace key. When you press the Backspace key, your computer beeps, because pressing the Backspace key when you're in 1-2-3 READY mode is an error.

You also can make your computer beep with a macro. Not only that—you can make your computer beep in four different tones! And if you're musically inclined, you can create a macro that makes your computer play a song whenever you want it to.

When you write a macro, there may be a point when you want to get the user's attention. The beep works great for that. Also, a beep is very effective to note the beginning or end of a macro.

Using the {BEEP} Command

The {BEEP} advanced macro command is the command you use in a macro to make the computer beep. You can make the computer beep in different tones by providing a number from 1 to 4 after the keyword BEEP. For example, {BEEP 2} produces a computer beep in tone 2. Note the space between the BEEP keyword and the number 2.

Retrieve the LAYOUT worksheet and save the worksheet with the name BEEP. Figure 14.1 shows a macro that plays each of the four available tones. You may recognize the pause {?} command from Chapter 11. Create, name, and document the macro, as shown in figure 14.1.

Making the Computer Beep

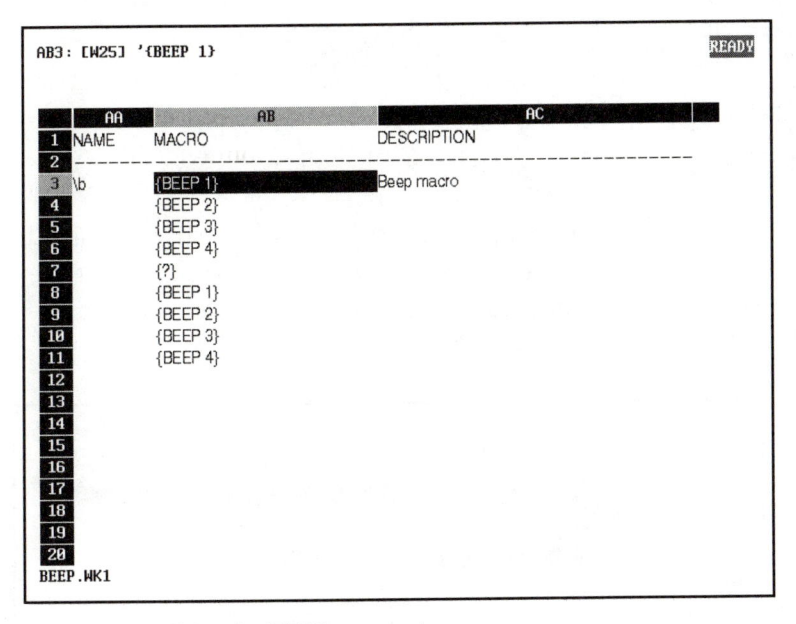

```
AB3: [W25] '{BEEP 1}                                    READY

          AA          AB                    AC
    1  NAME       MACRO               DESCRIPTION
    2  ---------------------------------------------------
    3   \b        {BEEP 1}            Beep macro
    4             {BEEP 2}
    5             {BEEP 3}
    6             {BEEP 4}
    7             {?}
    8             {BEEP 1}
    9             {BEEP 2}
   10             {BEEP 3}
   11             {BEEP 4}
   12
   13
   14
   15
   16
   17
   18
   19
   20
   BEEP.WK1
```

Fig. 14.1 Using the {BEEP} command.

Now, let's run the macro. Press **Alt-B** to start the macro. Tones 1 through 4 sound, respectively, and then the macro pauses. Press **Enter** to hear tones 1 through 4 again.

When you create a macro, you can use the {BEEP} command to remind the user to do something. And, as I mentioned earlier, if you're musically inclined, you may even be able to write a song by using the {BEEP} command.

OOPS! You must make sure that the beep sound is active when you use 1-2-3 Releases 2.3, 2.4, and 3.x. The beep is on by default, but some people turn off the beep because they find it distracting. You turn on the beep by selecting the **/W**orksheet **G**lobal **D**efault **O**ther **B**eep **Y**es command.

155

Using the {BEEP} Command in a User Input Macro

The {Beep} command is especially useful to alert the user of something on-screen. We're going to adapt the user input macro so that it beeps each time it pauses for input. Retrieve the INPUT file. The macro should appear as in figure 14.2.

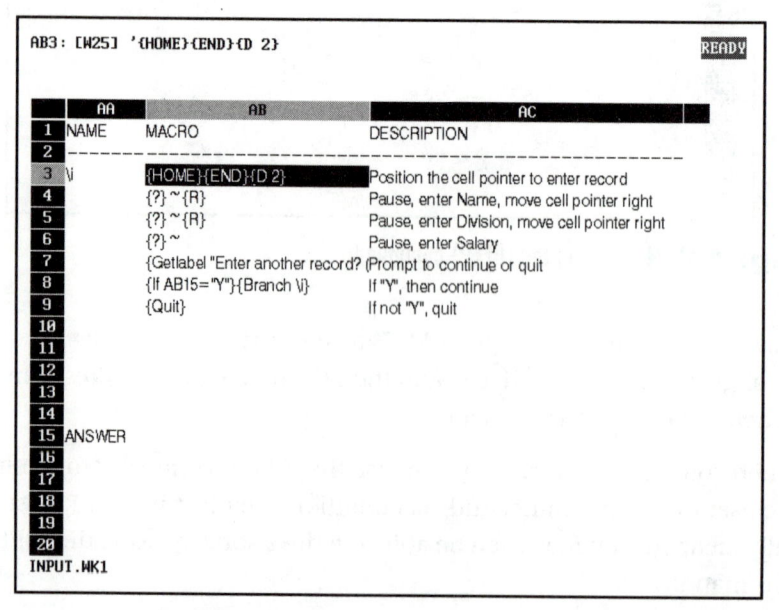

```
AB3: [W25] '{HOME}{END}{D 2}                                          READY

        AA          AB                          AC
1    NAME        MACRO                       DESCRIPTION
2    -------------------------------------------------------------------
3    \i          {HOME}{END}{D 2}            Position the cell pointer to enter record
4                {?}~{R}                     Pause, enter Name, move cell pointer right
5                {?}~{R}                     Pause, enter Division, move cell pointer right
6                {?}~                        Pause, enter Salary
7                {Getlabel "Enter another record? (Prompt to continue or quit
8                {If AB15="Y"}{Branch \i}    If "Y", then continue
9                {Quit}                      If not "Y", quit
10
11
12
13
14
15   ANSWER
16
17
18
19
20
INPUT.WK1
```

Fig. 14.2 The INPUT file macro.

You may remember from the last chapter that this macro positions the cell pointer and pauses for input for each column of data. The macro then prompts you to enter another record. We will add the {BEEP} commands to the ends of lines 1, 2, 3, and 4; this action will make the macro beep every time the macro pauses for input. Figure 14.3 shows the changed macro.

Making the Computer Beep

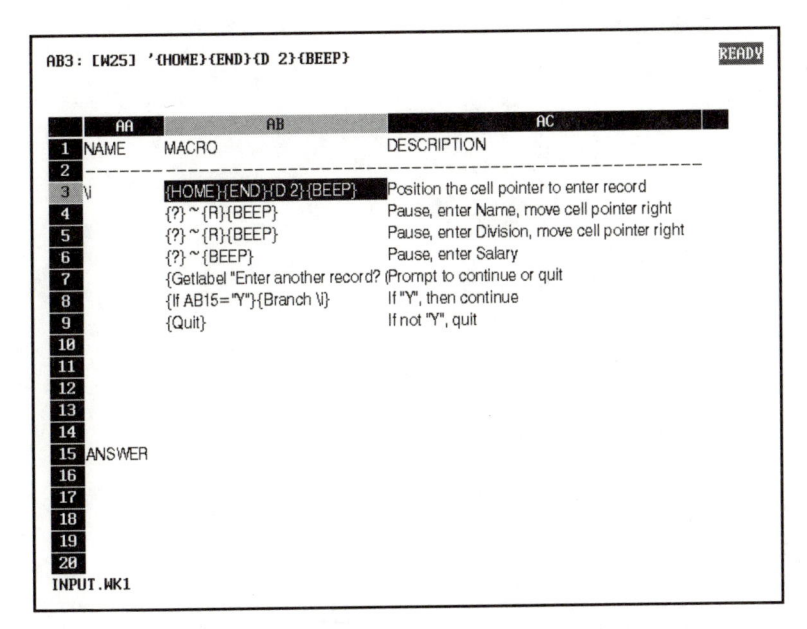

```
AB3: [W25] '{HOME}{END}{D 2}{BEEP}                              READY

        AA          AB                      AC
   1  NAME        MACRO                   DESCRIPTION
   2  ---------------------------------------------------------
   3  \I          {HOME}{END}{D 2}{BEEP}  Position the cell pointer to enter record
   4              {?}~{R}{BEEP}           Pause, enter Name, move cell pointer right
   5              {?}~{R}{BEEP}           Pause, enter Division, move cell pointer right
   6              {?}~{BEEP}              Pause, enter Salary
   7              {Getlabel "Enter another record? (Prompt to continue or quit
   8              {If AB15="Y"}{Branch \I} If "Y", then continue
   9              {Quit}                  If not "Y", quit
  10
  11
  12
  13
  14
  15  ANSWER
  16
  17
  18
  19
  20
INPUT.WK1
```

Fig. 14.3   The INPUT macro with the {BEEP} commands added.

Now run the macro. When the macro pauses for input, the computer beeps. This beep alerts you to the fact that you're supposed to do something.

Congratulations! You're now wily in the ways of Lotus macros. Well, maybe not wily yet, but you're certainly on your way to handling macros. Now that you're done with the book, don't you wish you had known about macros earlier? Most people do!

157

Index

Symbols

\ (backslash) in macros, 15
{?} (pause) advanced macro command, 116
    changing column widths, 122-125
    data entry, simplifying, 125-132
    erasing cells, 116-119
    formatting numbers, 119-122

A

activating LEARN mode, 71
/Add-In Attach command, 89
/Add-In Invoke command, 90
add-ins, 88
adding Macro Library Manager, 88-91
advanced macro commands, 112-114
    {?} (pause), 116
        changing column widths, 122-125
        data entry, simplifying, 125-132
        erasing cells, 116-119
        formatting numbers, 119-122
    {BEEP}, 154
        in user input macros, 156-157
    {BRANCH \i}, 137
    {GETLABEL}, 137-138
    {IF}, 138
        @CELLPOINTER function with, 147-151
        operators with, 144-147
Alt-*letter* macros, 20-21

anchored cell pointers, 118
arguments, 113

B

backslash (\) in macros, 15
{BEEP} advanced macro command, 154
    in user input macros, 156-157
{BRANCH \i} advanced macro command, 137

C

@CELLPOINTER function, 147-151
cells
    erasing, 116-119
        data from single cells, 24-27
        data from range of cells, 27-30
    format, changing, 50-53
    macro cell instructions, 139
characters, missing, 67
column widths
    changing, 32-42, 122-125
    default, 32
commands
    /Add-In Attach, 89
    /Add-In Invoke, 90
    advanced macro, 112-114
    erasing from macros, 139
    /File Directory, 79
    /File Save, 76
    /Range Erase, 19, 30, 60
    /Range Name Create, 16, 21
    /Range Name Labels Right, 16
    /Worksheet Column Column Range, 38

Index

/Worksheet Column Set-Width, 13
/Worksheet Erase, 95
/Worksheet Erase Yes Yes, 93-94
/Worksheet Global Default Other Beep Yes, 155
/Worksheet Global Default Other Undo Enable Quit, 67
/Worksheet Learn Range, 71, 76, 79
creating
  macro libraries, 91-94
  macros, 12-13
    guidelines, 18

D

data entry, simplifying, 125-132
default column widths, 32

E

editing macro libraries, 94-97
entering
  data, simplifying with macros, 125-132
  macros, 14-15
  names on worksheets, 12
erasing
  cells, 116-119
    data from single cells, 24-27
    data from range of , 27-30
  commands from macros, 139
errors, common macro errors, 66-67

F-G

file directories, changing, 78-80
/File Directory command, 79
/File Save command, 76
formatting
  numbers, 119-122
  ranges, 44-49
  worksheets, 50-53
function, @CELLPOINTER, 147-151
{GETLABEL} advanced macro commands, 137-138

I-K

{IF} advanced macro command, 138
  @CELLPOINTER function with, 147-151
  operators with, 144-147
keywords, 112

L

labels, 18
laying out macros, 13
LEARN mode, 70-71
  activating, 71
  recording macros with
    changing file directory, 78-80
    saving worksheets, 76-78
    typing name, city, state, 72-76
Learn range, 70
libraries, macro
  creating, 91-94
  editing, 94-97
  loading into memory, 98
  removing from memory, 97
loading macro libraries into memory, 98

161

Easy 1-2-3 Macros

M

Macro Library Manager, 88
   adding, 88-91
   menu, 92
macros, 8-9
   adding documentation to cell instructions, 139
   advanced macro commands, 112-114
      {?} (pause), 116-132
      {BRANCH \i}, 137
      {GETLABEL}, 137-138
      {IF}, 138, 144-151
      {BEEP}, 154-157
   Alt-*letter*, 20-21
   @CELLPOINTER function, 147-151
   changing file directories, 78-80
   column widths
      changing, 32-42, 122-125
      default, 32
   common errors, 66-67
   creating, 12-13
      guidelines, 18
   entering, 14-15
      name and address, 104-107
   erasing
      commands, 139
      cells, 116-119
      data from range of cells, 27-30
      data from single cells, 24-27
   formatting
      numbers, 119-122
      ranges, 44-49
      worksheets, 50-53
   isolating mistakes, 58-59, 62-63
   laying out, 13
   LEARN mode, 70-71
   libraries
      creating, 91-94
      editing, 94-97
      loading into memory, 98
      removing from memory, 97
   multitasking, *see* multitasking macros
   naming, 15-16
      descriptive names, 21-22
      guidelines, 19
   pausing, 116-132
      changing column widths, 122-125
      data entry, simplifying, 125-132
      erasing cells, 116-119
      formatting numbers, 119-122
      querying user, 136
   placing, 13-14
   printing worksheets with footers/page numbers, 107-109
   recording in 1-2-3 Release 3.x, 80-85
   running, 17-18, 140-142
      guidelines, 19
   saving worksheets, 76-78
   STEP mode, 58-59, 62-66
   typing
      name, city, state, 72-76
      name on worksheet, 12
   undoing effects, 67-68
   user input macros, 125-132
      {BEEP} advanced macro command in, 156-157
   writing, 12

Index

memory
  loading macro libraries into, 98
  removing macro libraries from, 97
menu, Macro Library Manager, 92
mistakes, isolating in macros, 58-59, 62-63
modes
  LEARN, 70-71
    activating, 71
    changing file directories with, 78-80
    saving worksheets with, 76-78
    typing name, city, state with, 72-76
  STEP, 58-59, 62-66
multitasking macros
  entering names and addresses, 104-107
  printing worksheets with footers/page numbers, 107-109

N-O

name and address, entering, 104-107
naming macros, 15-16
  descriptive names, 21-22
  guidelines, 19

P-Q

pausing macros, 116-132
  changing column widths, 122-125
  data entry, simplifying, 125-132
  erasing cells, 116-119
  formatting numbers, 119-122
  querying user, 136
placing macros, 13-14
planning macros, 13
printing worksheets with footers/page numbers, 107-109

R

/Range Erase command, 19, 30, 60
/Range Name Create command, 21, 16
/Range Name Labels Right command, 16
ranges
  erasing data from range of cells with macros, 27-30
  formatting numbers, 44-49
  Learn, 70
  names, 44
record buffers, 80
recording macros in 1-2-3 Release 3.x, 80-85
Release 3.x Record feature, 80-85
running macros, 17-18, 140-142
  guidelines, 19
  user input macros, 129-130

S

saving worksheets, 76-78
spaces, incorrectly placing, 67
spelling mistakes, 67
STEP mode, 58-59, 62-66

T

typing
    name, city, state, 72-76
    name on worksheet, 12

U-V

unanchored cell pointers, 118
undoing macros, 67-68
user input macros, 125-132
    {BEEP} advanced macro
      command in, 156-157

W-Z

/Worksheet Column Column
  Range command, 38
/Worksheet Column
  Set-Width, 13
/Worksheet Erase command, 95
/Worksheet Erase Yes Yes
  command, 93-94
/Worksheet Global Default Other
  Beep Yes command, 155
/Worksheet Global Default Other
  Undo Enable Quit command,
  67
/Worksheet Learn Range
  command, 71, 76, 79
worksheets
    changing format of numbers,
      145-147
    entering name on, 12
    formatting, 50-53
    printing with footers/page
      numbers, 107-109
    saving, 76-78
writing macros, 12